GEM-STONES OF THE SEVEN RAYS

GEM-STONES
OF THE
SEVEN RAYS

BY

C. NELSON STEWART, M.A.

Often in the lowly being dwells a hidden god ;
And like a nascent Eye covered by the eyelids
A pure spirit grows beneath the rugged skin of stones.

Gerard de Nerval

WILDSIDE PRESS

PREFACE

THE doctrine that one of the Seven Rays of life, or seven types of force, dwells in every form is clearly recognisable in the writings of Cornelius Agrippa, and also bears a strong likeness to the Astrological conception of planetary rulers. In modern Theosophical studies we find a somewhat fuller development of the same basic Idea, particularly in regard to human beings ; so that, if the medical man assures you your body belongs to one or other of the four blood-types, just as definitely does the occultist tell you that the spirit expressing himself in that body belongs to one of the seven ray-types.

To the ceremonialist and student of magic, precious stones are especially valuable as wave-meters transmitting specialised psychic qualities, and this little book groups some forty-seven mineral species and varieties under the Seven Rays. The main physical features are given for each stone, and in most cases some historical or ethnological notes are added, often with a bearing on the Ray quality of the stone.

In addition, the preliminary chapters gather together modern Theosophical statements regarding the Mineral Kingdom.

CONTENTS

CHAPTER I

CRYSTALS

MORE than thirty years ago an enthusiastic worker among precious stones wrote : " You know, I suppose, that there are spirits in stones—colour demons that mesmerise you ; pay them respect enough and they'll speak to you—they will begin to move, to twinkle, to gesticulate, sometimes even they come out, only beware that you conjure them back again. Every jewel you set must have its colour-scheme, every jewel must be treated as a painter would treat his picture." He was writing whimsically, of course, and yet there is something of the intuition of the true artist in his expressions. The brilliancy, the colour, and the symmetrical crystal forms of precious stones have in all ages suggested to man some kind of in-dwelling life, an idea that " precious stones are flowers that grow underground."

When we turn to physical facts, however, we find that we have no grounds for rushing to an easy con-clusion that a crystal is a " living " thing. Many crystals, it is true, appear to grow in a concentrated solution of their own substance. The general appearance and relative proportions of the parts remain the same while the bulk increases. But this is also true of a rubbish tip or a sand-dune, where you have particles settling down to a state of equilibrium between gravity and friction. In the crystal—the characteristic form of the mineral kingdom—we have a state of acquiescence, as it were, in presence of molecular forces. In the living organism, on the other hand, there is no static equilibrium as its goal, and we find it accumulating energy instead. We might conveniently picture a crystal as built up of a great number of tiny magnets, the shape of these and the number of poles varying with the substance of the mineral. Thus we might have one crystal with units or molecules of two poles, others with three, six, or eight, and always the molecules would interlock positive and negative poles as do the north and south poles of two steel magnets brought together. Obviously we should have different types of structure in the mineral substances thus built up, depending upon the build or space-pattern of the chemical molecules and atoms used.

We are now arriving at an important truth in mineralogy, namely, that the characteristic thing about crystal structure is not the geometrical faces we can see with the naked eye, but the regular arrangement of the ultra-microscopic chemical atoms which make up this type of substance. A mineral may have crystal structure and yet appear quite shapeless. Study a piece of granite, and you will see that the

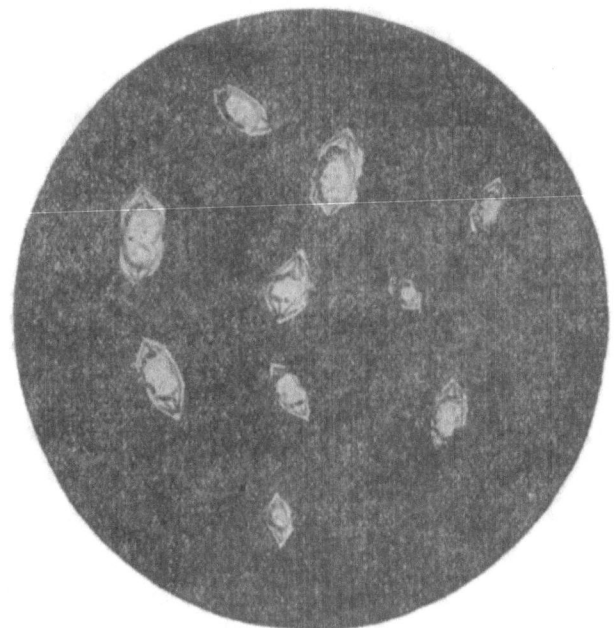

FIG. 1

hard glassy quartz is irregularly scattered through the rock. The glistening mica and the greyish or pinkish felspar show some clear signs of crystal shape because they seized the elbow-room first in the cooling of the molten rock or "magma." The quartz, cooling last, had to be content with the very irregular and branching holes and crannies left by the others, and yet it is crystalline in its structure.

There is a very beautiful and impressive illustration of the same fact in a famous British sandstone—Penrith sandstone. The quartz grains of this sandstone have been rubbed round and smooth in bygone ages, then pressed into rock, and water containing silica (which is quartz) has soaked through the mass at some time.

If we rub off a grain or two and look at them under a low-power microscope we see that a wonderful thing has happened. Each rounded grain has gathered to itself silica from the water and built up a tiny crystal with itself as nucleus. We can trace the roughly spherical outline of the somewhat stained original sand-grain and round it is the transparent new quartz with its crystal outline. The two hexagonal pyramids are there in minute perfection. Rounded and disguised though it was in the sand-grain state, each particle was still crystalline, and so when the opportunity came it completed itself quite inevitably. There is a curious thrill for the imaginative in thinking about this ancient rock-mass of quartz grains which has achieved perfection in all its individual members after unknown ages; the dismembered body of Osiris is once more complete in each tiny particle.

Crystallinity, then, is a matter of structure not shape. Maskelyne's definition of a crystal was '' a system of molecules belonging to an individual substance symmetrically arranged and presenting the same properties along all lines taken parallel to the same direction, or to directions that are similarly disposed in respect to symmetrically repeated features.'' Groth simplified this still further. Elasticity, he argued, was a term which would describe the degree of resistance of a substance to the passage of any type of physical energy—light, heat, electricity, magnetism, and so on; and his definition of a crystal was, a solid body the elasticity of which is equal in parallel directions, but which on the other hand is different in different directions.

Symmetry in crystals, it will be gathered, is not the same as geometrical symmetry. In geometrical symmetry we have an object which it is possible to split into halves or thirds, quarters, or some still smaller fractions, which will be identical in measurements and the relation of their parts. The planes of symmetry along which a particular crystal may be divided do not necessarily give equal parts, but the relationship between the faces (the angles) and the properties (hardness, conductivity to heat, lustre, etc.,) of these faces are identical in symmetrically related parts. Again it is the minute structure which is the whole basis of crystal properties.

As an illustration it may be helpful to think of a log of wood. However you may cut it,—cross-grain, or along the grain—the fundamental possibilities of the wood remain. Or take a square of soldiers drawn up on the forming-fours principle. You may take away a corner of the square, or cut it to a triangle or some irregular shape, but each trained man occupies a position which has no relation to the new outline but only to the original square; and on the command, " Form two deep ", his movements will be calculated independently of the new mass outline. The movements in this case we might say are determined by two lines at right angles—two rectangular " axes."

Scientific study of crystal structure has given us the Seven Crystal Systems, which are again subdivided according to the degree of completeness of symmetry into thirty-two classes. Without going into the detail which can be got from any text-book on crystallography, we may state these shortly in a series passing from the least symmetrical types to the most perfect.

THE SEVEN CRYSTAL SYSTEMS

1. TRICLINIC :   Three unequal axes (a : b : c) inclined otherwise than at 90°, 60°, 45°, 30°.

2. MONOCLINIC : Three unequal axes (a : b : c) two inclined but *b* perpendicular to the other two.

3. RHOMBIC :   Three unequal but rectangular axes (a : b : c).

4. TETRAGONAL : Three rectangular axes, two equal but the vertical axis different (a : a : c).

5. TRIGONAL ;   Three equal and equally inclined axes (a : a : a).

6. HEXAGONAL : Three equal axes lying in the same plane and inclined at 60° to each other, and a fourth axis, the vertical axis, perpendicular to them and unequal. This latter is a hexagonal axis of symmetry (a : a : a : c).

7. CUBIC :   Three equal rectangular axes (a : a : a).

We must note briefly here the important modern advance in the study of crystal-structure through the use of the X-rays. The origin of the method was a discovery by Laue in 1912, but the main honour lies with Sir William L. Bragg for its subsequent develop- ment. To take a rough analogy, we might say that the exceedingly short wave-length of the radiations from an X-ray tube as compared with the length of visible light waves, permits the X-rays to penetrate the meshwork of the crystal to varying depths before reflection from the molecule, much as if indiarubber peas (X-rays) as contrasted with ordinary tennis balls (light) were to be projected against a series of taut tennis nets one behind the other. Using a fine penci of X-rays of known lengths—got by enclosing the tube in a box with a slit—and projecting them on the surface of a crystal, the angle and intensity of the various reflections is detected by the measurable electrical (ionising) effect on a gas such as sulphur dioxide or methyl bromide. From these data calcula- tions can be made giving the spatial arrangement of the molecules composing the crystal.

*   *   *   *

Thus far, in trying to underline some of the charac- teristics of this kingdom of nature, we have perhaps emphasised the view that crystals are non-living. It would be, however, entirely out of accord with the general purpose of our study if we were to close this chapter without going a little deeper.

The occult philosopher sees that both the materialist and the vitalist are right as far as they go. He sees but One Life in point of origin and " substance ", yet Three in point of time and mode of motion—self-conscious, matter-building, and form building. The vitalist gleans evidence for the presence of the form-building type, and rightly feels rather than proves that the whole is somehow greater than its cellular parts with all their complex chemistry and physics.

Professor Schafer in his famous address to the British Association [1] declared that problems of life are problems of matter. " The more we study the manifestations of life, the more we become convinced of the truth of this statement and the less we are disposed to call in the aid of a special and unknown form of energy to explain those manifestations." He pointed out that all or nearly all the movements and reactions of simple living creatures were imitable by suitably arranged surface tensions, osmosis, colloids and so on ; that crystals give examples of growth and reproduction, and even have a limit of growth in most

[1] *The Nature, Origin, and Maintenance of Life*, 1912.

cases as in organisms. Cell-division or karyokinesis could be imitated with a sodium chloride solution containing carbon particles in suspension " which arrange and rearrange themselves under the influence of the mòvements of the electrolytes in a manner indistinguishable from that adopted by the particles of chromatin in a dividing nucleus." He holds that evolution is universal, even in the chemical elements.

The Professor is content to start with matter, not so the philosopher, Let us hear Schopenhauer :

The tendency to gravitation in a stone is as unexplainable as thought in a human brain. If matter can—no one knows why—fall to the ground, then it can also—no one knows why—think. . . . As soon, even in mathematics, as we trespass beyond the purely mathematical, as soon as we reach the inscrutable, adhesion, gravitation, and so on, we are faced by phenomena which are to our senses as mysterious as the will and thought of man. . . . If you consider that there is in a human form some sort of a *spirit*, then you are obliged to concede the same to a stone. If your dead, utterly passive matter can manifest a tendency towards gravitation, or like electricity, attract and repel and send out sparks—then, as well as the brain, it can also think. In short, every particle of the so-called spirit we can replace with an equivalent of matter, and every particle of matter replace with spirit. . . . Thus it is not the Cartesian division of things into matter and spirit that can ever be found philosophically exact ; but if we divide them into *will* and *manifestation*, which form of division has naught to do with the former, for it spiritualises everything all that which is in the first instance real and objective—body and matter—it transforms into a representation, and every manifestation into will.

Madame Blavatsky, writing in 1887, stated the occultist's position in clear terms :

Chemical Science may well say that there is no difference between the matter which composes the ox and that which forms man. But the Occult doctrine is far more explicit. It says : Not only the chemical compounds are the same, but the same infinitesimal *invisible* Lives compose the atoms of the bodies of the mountain and the daisy, of man and the ant, of the elephant and the tree which shelters it from the sun. Each particle—whether you call it organic or inorganic —*is a* Life.[1]

We must note carefully that she is not saying that the consciousness of a man, or an ant, or a daisy, is any kind of summation of these infinitesimal lives : that is rather Professor Schafer's idea, if we make the tiny units cells instead of atoms. She is asserting the sameness of the life-pulse behind matter as matter. What occult sm has to say about the life-pulse developing in the mineral kingdom we shall see in the next chapter.

[1] *The Secret Doctrine*, 1893 Edn. I, 281. Adyar Edn I, 305.

CHAPTER II

OCCULT MINERALOGY

'' THREEFOLD are beings : animate, green-growing or vegetable (as plants), and still (as stones and metals),'' said the Hebraist Kimchi in the twelfth century.[1] Our own Sir Thomas Browne, with his inimitable luxuriance of words, puts in a plea for the minerals as a humble form of life. For, he says :

Though Moses have left us no mention of minerals, nor made any other description than suits unto the apparent and visible creation, yet is there, unquestionably, a very large class of creatures in the earth far above the condition of elementarity. And, although not in a distinct and indisputable way of vivency, or answering in all points the properties and affections of plants, yet in inferior and descending constitutions they do, like these, contain specific distinctions, and are determined by seminalities, that is, created and defined seeds committed unto the earth from the beginning. Wherein, although they attain not the indubitable requisites of animation, yet have they a near affinity thereto.

---

[1] " Entia triplicia sunt, animatum, virescens (vegetabile, ut plantae) et silens (ut lapides et metalla)," *Comm. on Jer.*, X, 8. David Kimchi (1160-1235) Jewish grammarian and commentator who lived at Narbonne in the south of France and wrote a lexicon and grammar used by all later writers.

Occult philosophy today finds a place for the mineral kingdom in the great sweeping outlines of its evolutionary scheme, not only granting it an indwelling life, but chronicling the earlier stages of the life now dreaming in the minerals of our particular planet and forecasting its immensely remote future. The thoroughgoing materialist like Professor Schafer is not far off the truth in his conception of a life gradually increasing its expression from the atom to the mineral, from the mineral to ultra-microscopic bacteria, thence to visible bacteria and single-celled organisms, and so up and up the mighty ladder of progress. Only, his time-scale is ludicrously out and much of his inference mistaken. What is now the consciousness of a man may have been in the unthinkably remote past the primitive appetites and shrinking of a lowly cell or the vague thrillings of a mineral shape, but it is not the sum of the cells of the body in which it now presides ; nor was that in us which says " I " ever an animal or plant or stone. The powers you have of response to the outside world are truly a heritage from a long evolution, but you, the " I " or ego, took up that heritage as an undeveloped human being.

It will be understood that within the limits of a short chapter it is utterly impossible to refer to more than those parts of the occult scheme of evolution immediately bearing upon our subject, and to grasp even these intelligently requires supplementary reading, much as if one were writing a detailed study of say, the chemical element Boron, and, in doing so, taking for granted that the reader is well acquainted with the periodic classification of the elements and its groups and affinities.

The great unit is a solar system : a life-giving sun with life-bearing planets revolving round it. In spite of the scientific opinion of the moment, the occultist asserts that a sun easily outlasts one set of planets. True, there are " schemes " of evolution, definite areas where special evolutionary work is carried on in historical continuity from an old planet to a new one. Again, there is the novel idea of invisible planets attached to each of these schemes, where preliminary work and finishing work are carried out in materials incalculably more sensitive than physical matter.

There must be, of course, from the earliest stages, Will and Life inherent in the atoms, but the life which battles its way upwards through myriad forms comes in great pulses or waves at very long intervals of time. It dwells first in those invisible worlds where form can scarcely bind it, and, in its thirst for defined, clear contact with something outside itself it works its way

slowly into denser forms of matter, traversing the
"three elemental kingdoms" with their protean
shapes.   The next step brings it to the physical world,
where it is tied down hand and foot in the mineral,
faintly aware of violent physical impacts, of fire and
electricity.   Earthquake and volcano, steam and water,
even man with his smelting and hammering and roll-
ing, all play their part in sending vibrations to the
life within, so that in the course of ages it becomes
dimly conscious of a "without," and graduates in
the next cycle to some humble form of plant.

All this does not happen without the help of intelligences other than the Supreme Mind. Since there are,
and have been, other solar systems there is no difficulty
about a staff even at the outset, and the same applies
to planetary schemes.   Having already declared our
heresy in the matter of astronomy, we may
blithely continue with the statement that the moon
is the predecessor of the earth—in fact that is how
moons are usually supplied to a new planet : it is the
body of the ancestor—

Prajâpati

> Art Thou, and 'tis to Thee
> They knelt in worshipping the old world's far light,
> The first of mortal men.

Our mineral kingdom, that is, the life now expressing itself through it, was the third elemental kingdom

of the moon. From our point of view it was not in objective existence, being astral in its material. Our present corresponding elemental matter is seen by clairvoyants as the luminous fluidic matter which is thrown into form and movement by desire and emotion. Psycho-analysis has shown us unwittingly one section of the fauna of this region, and substantially vindicated Paracelsus' description of living things created by long-standing desires and suppressed passions.

Referring back, the successive pulses or life-waves will be recollected, occurring throughout a scheme of evolution like the orderly pressure wave from a great heart. There are seven of these running parallel on earth and the oldest is naturally that in which we, as human minds, are carried along. In addition there are the animal, vegetable, mineral and three elemental kingdoms.

After the rest-period following the lunar evolution, began the preliminary work for our system. Including the invisible centres in space the earth system has seven " globes," technically referred to under the letters A to G, the earth being D, midmost in the series. Beings from the moon evolution wrought at the invisible patterns for the forms of the forthcoming evolution, laying down lines of force and axes and fashioning archetypes. This epoch is known as the first Round.

There have been other periods of activity with intervals of repose and we are now in the fourth Round.

This first Round particularly concerns us, for working from globe to globe, when " the seventh Globe is reached . . . the whole germinal mineral kingdom is formed, although formed only in filmy shapes, not minerals as you know them . . . but always as glowing gaseous masses ; everything that now exists in the mineral kingdom is found on the last Globe of that first Round."

We may sum up their task by saying that on Globe A they give the seven archetypal forms for each kingdom ; on Globe B they multiply forms containing the essentials of each archetype ; on Globe C they densify these forms ; on Globe D they shape them in yet denser matter ; on Globe E they make them more complex and slightly refine them ; on Globe F they build them of finer matter ; on Globe G they finally perfect them. This is the method in every Round.[1]

From the standpoint of the psychic investigator the life-pulse behind the mineral kingdom, explains Mr. Leadbeater, will take its rise at a level depending upon his powers of vision, up to the insight of the Adept who would perceive " that the force which entered into and worked through all these successive veils came in reality from outside this cosmic-prakritic

[1] Besant, *The Pedigree of Man*, p. 58 et seq.

plane altogether, and was in truth simply one of the manifestations of the Divine Force." [1]

At the same time the subject has its complexities for the occult student because of the parallel evolutions we have mentioned. The general reader will catch the drift of the following quotation if he will bear in mind that what we have been calling a life-pulse is here named monadic essence :

> It must be borne in mind that monadic essence at one stage of its evolution towards humanity manifests through the elemental kingdom, while at a later stage it manifests through the mineral kingdom ; but the fact that two bodies of monadic essence at these different stages are in manifestation at the same moment, and that one of these manifestations (the earth elemental) occupies the same space as and inhabits the other (say a rock), in no way interferes with the evolution either of one or the other, nor does it imply any relation between the bodies of monadic essence lying within both. The rock will also be permeated by its appropriate variety of the omnipresent life-principle, but that is again totally distinct from either of the essences above mentioned." [2]

We may now ask what occult science has to say upon the question of the supposed virtues of precious stones, whose bewildering and motley catalogue in the old writers led Sir Thomas Browne to complain that " he must have more heads than Rome had

[1] *The Devachanic Plane*, p. 90. The atomic sub-plane is the carrier at each level.

[2] *The Astral Plane*, p. 75.

hills, that makes out half of those virtues ascribed unto stones, and their not only medical but magical properties." We learn that certain precious stones, like some woods and gums used in incense, have a vibration naturally corresponding with the vibration rates of some of the higher emotions. To carry one on the person is somewhat like having with you a tiny tuning-fork which is continually sounding a pure musical note. " A stone, the particles of which move naturally on the physical plane in a key which is identical at this level with the key of purity on high levels, will itself, even without magnetisation, operate as a check upon impure thought or feeling by virtue of its overtones ; and furthermore, it can be readily charged at astral or mental levels with the undulations of pure thought or feeling which are set in the same key."

The jewel represents the highest development of the mineral kingdom, and consequently its power of receiving and retaining impressions is much greater than is the case with almost any other object. The Gnostic gems employed in initiation ceremonies two thousand years ago still remain vigorous centres of magnetic influence, as may be seen and felt by any sensitive person who will take the trouble to examine some of those in the British Museum.[1]

We shall return to this topic of the occult uses of precious stones in the next chapter.

[1] *The Hidden Side of Things*, pp. 404, 413.

There is another fact worthy of mention which has been disclosed by clairvoyant research: many precious stones have permanent atoms attached to them. A permanent atom is a special atom linked to a little pool of divine life which one day becomes the spirit in man. Every human body contains one—a physical atom which has been in each of the bodies worn by the immortal reincarnating ego, and about us in the various living forms of nature are distributed great numbers of these specialised atoms, each with its overshadowing divine life seeking a bridge to reach the worlds of dense matter, each destined in some future cycle to be the physical plane nucleus of a human being. This no doubt was the secret behind the curious ancient Jewish idea of the bone called Luz—a mysterious indestructible little bone somewhere in the body. It is even said to have been produced before a royal personage and its indestructibility demonstrated both by the hammer on an anvil and by fire. Some located it in the coccyx, others in the higher vertebrae, some in the Wormian bones of the skull.

Dr. Besant says,

We find permanent atoms scattered through the mineral and vegetable kingdoms, but are unable to pierce to the reasons which govern their distribution. A permanent atom may be found in a pearl, in a ruby, in a diamond; many may be found scattered through veins of ore, and so on.   On the other hand much mineral does not seem to contain any.[1]

One speculates whether the sort of personality that gathers about famous jewels with a long history owes something to the presence of a permanent atom, which, in turn, from this association would reap a richly varied harvest of vibrational experience, especially when used in ceremonials.

We have not considered the development of the mineral Group-Soul.   This is a highly technical subject which it would be unwise to attempt to condense in these pages, as the result would be mere jargon to those encountering the idea for the first time.   It will suffice to refer to A Study in Consciousness for a masterly description, and to extract here, as useful to the student, the point that in the case of the mineral Group-Soul the lowest envelope is of etheric or atomic physical matter.   Hence :

> The laws of space—apart from the specialisation of the contents of the Group-Soul, the permanent triads—may lead to a division of it.   Thus a vein of gold in Australia may lead to the inmineralisation of many such triads within a single envelope, while the laying down of another vein in a distant place, say the Rocky Mountains, may lead to the division of this envelope, and the transfer of part of its contents to America in their own envelope.[2]

[1] A Study in Consciousness, p. 127, which see for further explanation of the permanent atom.

[2] A Study in Consciousness, pp. 116-7.

CHAPTER III

THE SEVEN RAYS

WHEN the occult philosopher has to deal with some part of the objective world he is in the position of one who has travelled to a far country and on his return tries to communicate his experiences. His power of explanation is from the outset limited by the comprehension of his hearers, who are able to follow him only as far as their own experience supplies analogies and associated ideas. In regard to, say, the mineral kingdom, the occultist's outlook differs from that of any other type of thinker because he is not concerned solely, nor even primarily, with physical details and characteristics. The astronomer is perhaps the only one among the students of visible things who approaches him in a sense of proportion and range of thought. He has continually in mind the living Unity behind the diversity, the Emanator of the beings thronged upon the Jacob's ladder which is His universe, nor can the occultist consider the present without the past leading to it and the future shaping from it. He is the heir of a tradition of the highest antiquity, undying as the germ-plasm itself, changing in forms perhaps, but still living on and expanding in fullness of knowledge ; and, in addition, he is a practical investigator and observer, so far as his powers will carry him, of the forces and structure of superphysical regions. Without disparaging or under-estimating the great work of physical science, he can accept and use it, adding the unknown factors which solve at least the general problems.

The geologist in his roughest classification might group the rocks of the earth according to their origin as igneous, sedimentary, and metamorphic ; but the occultist is more interested in regarding them as representing the qualities of the first, second, and third Logoi—the three Persons of the Trinity. The division, however, which most matters to men is the one we are now to consider—that is, according to the seven Rays ; for that is a division which places each man in rapport with sections of the manifested world below and above him.

We need not labour the point that the conception of the Seven Regents under the Trinity is ancient and widespread. In Hinduism, " Seven are the great Gods below the Trimurti. Five only are working and two concealed.   They are Indra, Vayu, Agni, Varuna, Kshiti."   In the *Book of Tobit* [1] Raphael declares : " I am Raphael, one of the seven holy angels, which present the prayers of the saints, and which go in and out before the glory of the Holy One."   They are the seven planetary rulers of the mediaeval astrologer, and direct the evolutions of the planetary schemes which bear their names.   But it is better to concentrate upon the idea that each has some part of His field of consciousness everywhere through- out the solar system ; wherever you have a certain type of motion, a certain colouring, a particular ideal for the unit living amongst its fellows, there is His department.   It is a matter of function not locality. A rough and ready comparison is the organised whole presented by a civilised community in which you have events, acts, processes, people, materials and methods, which can be classified as legal, medical, religious, artistic, commercial, and so on.   The in- dividual who is mainly concerned in administering law in the community is always a potential subject for medicine or commerce or religion, and he does not build his own house.

Thus in each of the Ray divisions—the Seven Rays of the One Light—we find members of all the

[1] xii, 15.

kingdoms of nature visible and invisible, perhaps with details of structure expressing the energy of another Ray. Each of the life-pulses or evolutionary waves discussed in the last chapter contains all seven types.

The German kabbalist and magician Cornelius Agrippa (1486-1535), expressed this doctrine of the Rays in a curiously involved passage :

> For this is the band and continuity of nature, that all superior virtue doth flow through every inferior with a long and continued series, dispersing its rays even to the very last thing : and inferiors, through their superiors, come to the very supreme of all. For as inferiors are successively joined to their superiors that there proceeds an influence from their head, the first cause, as a certain string stretched out, to the lowermost things of all : of which string if one end be touched, the whole doth presently shake, and such a touch doth sound to the other end. And at the motion of the inferior the superior also is moved, to which the other doth answer as strings in a lute well tuned.[1]

But we need not to-day follow the magician of the middle ages into the extravagances of the doctrine of sympathies, nor the primitive man into fetishism, through an irrational attempt to apply this theory. There are even modern writers on the occult who tend to give the impression that by tediously cultivating the right " conditions," and surrounding himself with material of this kind and that, the student taps the source of a kind of perpetual motion which will

---

[1] *De Occulta Philosophia*, I, 38.

3

bear him to Nirvana " free gratis." While philosophically it may be true that the life of the Lord of
the First Ray lies behind a diamond or a lion, a
warrior or a king, or an angel who directs earth-
quakes, obviously the wearing of a diamond or the
eating of a lion's heart will not—except in so far as it
is an effective suggestion—make a craven a hero.
On the other hand, it need not be doubted that
there is consonance or dissonance of vibrational rates
between man and natural objects sufficiently strong
to influence many sensitive people in a degree not
large in itself, but considerable when acting over long
periods. Even the average man is affected in this
way : we might instance for example the effect of
underlying soil and rock upon the physical appearance
(and probably psychic make-up as well) of those who
live upon them.

The numbering of the Rays from one to seven is
not arbitrary, their arrangement is such that natural
relationships are maintained, just as in the vertical
columns of the periodic table of the chemical elements. The first three Rays, often referred to as major
Rays, repeat in their qualities those of the Trinity :
will, wisdom and creative activity. In discussing all
the Rays the most feasible introduction is to describe
in a few words the human type ensouled by each.

The First Ray is distinguished by the will which its sons show as their supreme quality. Courage, strength and inflexibility, and the rare gift of appreciating the value of each individual are theirs. It is the Ray of the born warrior and ruler. Direct in its methods, headlong as Jove's thunderbolt, it reflects the Power of the Father. Baladeva or Hercules, Manu the lawgiver, and Moses are types of myth figures of this Ray, although every race and nation has lesser figures which capture the imagination of the people: an Alexander, a Hunyadi, a Bolivar; a Richard Coeur de Lion, Sir William Wallace, John of Arc, Bayard or Washington. Significantly, the hardest and most brilliant of all stones, the diamond, is its highest development in the mineral kingdom. The characteristic colour is electric blue.

Vishnu the Preserver, the love which is wisdom, marks out the Second Ray type. The unity and interdependence of all that lives becomes the master-thought of this, the great Teaching Ray. Like those of the First Ray its scions have a touch of nobility in their presence, a nobility springing from heart-wisdom and unselfish love; differing from the dignity of the power-with-honour of the First Ray. The Lord Buddha is the loftiest example of this expression of the divine

life ; and the Krishna of *The Bhagavad Gita,* the Lord
Christ, especially of some Gnostic gospels, stand with
Him.   A multitude of lesser names, like St. Francis of
Assisi, might be cited.   This is the indigo Ray, but
the student should remember that true colours
are seldom given out, and also that in passing
from one plane to another they are liable to be
reversed into their complementaries, as indigo into
orange.

The Third or Green Ray is that of creative activity
and has a correspondence with the Third Person of
the Trinity, the Holy Ghost. The First Ray may supply
the power and the Second the wise motive and loving
insight, but it is the Third which knows the materials
and calculates the stresses they will stand, how best
they may be arranged, and estimates the time required for the work.   The judge, the arbiter, the philosopher, are of this class intellectually, striving always to
take a whole view of a situation ; and on the practical
side we have the various " sons of Martha," the road
and railway engineer and the town-planner. The man
of this Ray has an instinct for times and seasons, for
the psychological moment, hence the world of finance
is his as well.   Adaptability and understanding are his
natural gifts ; and he might copy the fifteenth-century
Ludovico Sforza in his badge of the mulberry tree—

" symbol, in its long delay and sudden yielding of
flowers and fruit together, of a wisdom which econo-
mises all forces for an opportunity of sudden and sure
effect." Perhaps Aristotle as he appeared to Europe
of the middle ages is a good type of myth figure for
this Ray, a great encyclopaedic mind, the " master of
them that know."

The Third Ray from its very nature acts as focus and
director to the remainder, Four to Seven. A good
simile is the thumb opposing the four fingers. The
First Ray is like the clenched fist, the Second the
hand held out as a cup or support, the Third the
thumb with the four finger-tips gathered against it ;
then each finger extended in turn will represent the
remainder.

About the next Ray, the Fourth, clings an atmosphere which is both intensely human and exhilarating.
The Fourth Ray man is a seeker of harmony. Often
he will not see the how and why of things with the
profound intellectual grasp of the Third Ray, but he
is intuitively aware of the glorious rhythm and balance
the Logos maintains throughout His evolving universe,
and from time to time he touches an ecstasy in this
realisation of beauty. Himself by spiritual birth endowed as a potential creator of beauty and harmony,
he is God's enthusiastic audience, applauding from

the depths of his soul the perfect performance of the Great Artist in the mystery-drama of the worlds. Ebb and flow, positive thrust and negative pull, fascinate him alike in nature and man's civilisations, and he strives to feel behind it all the graceful pattern with its geometric setting that is God's thought. Orpheus is the great myth figure of the Ray, and in historical times Leonardo da Vinci is an excellent example.   Orange may be allotted as the Ray colour.

Entirely different in temperament, yet not so different in his quest, is the man of the Fifth Ray.   He too is seeking order in the universe around him, but his ideal is stability rather than rhythm, and he is interested more in form than in life.   The Fourth Ray man prefers to let the phases of the world-process pass through himself in order to know them ; the Fifth Ray man abhors the personal equation and as far as he can studies objects by the aid of other objects—nothing satisfies him better than to arrange for the subject of his attention to record its own reactions. He feels then that he is nearer the truth which is his ideal.   This is the Ray of concrete science and ordered knowledge. Its colour is the golden yellow of intellect. As myth figures we have Zoroaster in the east and Hermes Trismegistus (the Thoth of Egypt) reverenced by all the proto-scientists of the west. In the eighth verse of the legendary emerald tablet ascribed to the latter is written : " Ascend with the greatest sagacity from the earth to heaven, and then again descend to the earth, and unite together the powers of things superior and things inferior. Thus you will obtain the glory of the whole world, and obscurity will fly away from you." This is the scientific method : to start from the earth. Minor heroic figures there are, yet fewer than one might expect, for outside their own Ray their achievement is little realised, except in cases like Galileo, bowing as a personality to authority, though inwardly recognising only one authority—experimental observation—and murmuring " E pur se muove."

The keynote of the Sixth Ray is Bhakti, that utter devotion to a divine personality, or even to an abstract ideal, which can gather up all the forces of a human being in a lifetime of sustained effort. For many hundreds of years, until the last century or so, it has been the dominant Ray of western Europe, and its works are familiar to us. Between it and the Second Ray there is a basic sympathy. Both feel the divine Love, the major Ray in a sweet and impersonal way, " above the smoke and stir of this dim spot called Earth ; " the Sixth Ray man in a more

specialised and human fashion longs for direct relationship between the Deity and himself :

> The dying fish the careless angler took
> And cast on earth beside the rippling brook,
> Turns on the water no more longing glance
> Than I on Thee, oh grant me but a look.

To fit himself for this relationship he works hard at the
acquisition of purity and goodness.   The great figures
are Jesus Christ and the youthful Krishna.   Minor
figures hardly need be quoted from the great throng
of the past both in east and west—from the fiery
poet-mystics of Islam to the sin-conscious saint of
mediaeval Europe.   The colour for the Ray is a
crimson or rose-red.

The last Ray, the Seventh, is of special interest
because it is succeeding the Sixth as the dominant in
the world.   Beauty and purpose in skilled action
characterise it, so that it is spoken of as the Ceremonial Ray.   Borrowing the essence of all the Rays—
will, wisdom, philosophy, art, science and devotion—
the developed man of this Ray devises a scheme of
action which is precise, logical, harmonious and econo-
mical, and he particularly takes into account the
psychological and psychic factors, utilising the forces
of the invisible worlds by his ceremonies just as on the
material plane he erects wind and water mills.   On this
line contact is made with the great unseen evolution

of the Devas, familiar as the angels of Christen-
dom.   In the social organism the activity of the
Seventh Ray is best known meantime in Freemasonry
and its allied movements.   The greatest myth figure
of the Ray, though now faded out of the racial mind,
was Osiris in his aspect of King of the dead, " the
first of those who are in the West," in connection
with whose worship the elaborate Egyptian burial
ceremonial was evolved with its multiplicity of amulets.
In more recent times Proclus and Apollonius of Tyana
seem the best representatives ; and later still, adepts
like the Comte de St. Germain and Cagliostro.   This
Ray has a particular connection with the mineral kingdom which it uses in its magic.   Similarly the Sixth is
linked with the vegetable and the Fifth with the
animal kingdom.   There is also the less positive type
of Seventh Ray individual who is notable for his sensitiveness to nature and the spirits of nature, the Devas ;
some musicians for instance, and a rare literary genius
like the author of *The Centaur*, Maurice de Guérin.
The Ray colour is violet.

One's own Ray is not ascertained so easily as might be
thought. Astrology is a doubtful guide, as Doctor Robert
Fludd the Rosicrucian (1574-1637) stated long ago :

    I mention the Science of Genethlialogie, which treateth
of the Judgement of Nativities, wherein I produce the great

dispute between the two famous philosophers, Porphyrie and Iamblichus, whereof the first did hold that a man might come to the knowledge of his owne Genius or good Angell by the art of astrologie . . . Iamblichus his opinion was that a man had neede of the assistance and knowledge of a higher spirit than was any of those which were Governours of Fatalitie. . . . I seemed there to consent with Iamblichus, averring with him, that without the revelation of that high and heavenly Spirit, which was granted unto the Elect, none could come to the familiaritie or knowledge of his good Angell.[1]

The Ray of the inner, immortal man is not always evident in the accomplishments of the transient personality. Those who wish to follow up the question, however, would do well to consult Ernest Wood's admirable manual on *The Seven Rays.*

The precious and semi-precious stones of the Rays, apart from the scanty and confused hints in astrological and mystical tradition, were first stated by C. W. Leadbeater in his book on *The Science of the Sacraments,* and the chapters which follow are of the nature of a handbook to his list, with a number of tentative additions. A perusal of C. W. Leadbeater's work will show how in religious ceremonial precious stones are valuable foci or centres through which the special energies of the various Rays may be conducted by Deva helpers for the stimulation of a congregation of worshippers.

[1] *Squeesing of Parson Foster's Sponge,* II, 12.

In trying to grasp something of the essential qualities of the Rays it is not sufficient to memorise lists of types · which mainly express their respective qualities. We have to acquire some perception of the abstract modes of motion, so to speak, of the different Rays, as if each had a different wave-front and moulded matter accordingly. It is a useful exercise to draw up lists of materials or arts arranged under the seven types agreeably to one's own intuition of their natures, after meditating carefully upon groups known to be representative. The lists which you draw up will probably contain errors, like any schoolboy's essay ; still, in reaching after the abstract qualities of the Ray you have gained further knowledge of them, and the purpose of the exercise is fulfilled.

A word of caution is necessary. It is not suggested that you attempt to discover the real dominant Ray of any particular object or form of activity—that is a task for the trained occultist ; but you can sense in special qualities of each thing the influence of one of the Rays, just as a mediaeval astrologer might have said, " all swiftness is of Mercury, all beauty of Venus, all benevolence from Jupiter," although he did not know by tradition or observation the actual planetary ruler of the thing he contemplated.

An example or two will make this clearer. We pass rapidly in review the characteristics of the Rays as expressed in human consciousness—strength, wisdom, and so on—then perhaps visualise the jewels of the Rays with all we know of their qualities. Next we select a class of things like natural fluids or secretions and in turn pass them in review while trying to contact the essential nature of each, constantly referring to our set of seven abstract ideas in search of their parents and relatives. We may get a list something like this :

1st Ray	....	WATER
2nd Ray	....	MILK
3rd Ray	....	SEA-WATER
4th Ray	....	ALBUMEN, sperm and ovum
5th Ray	....	HONEY, pancreatic juice
6th Ray	...	BLOOD
7th Ray	....	WINE, hormones, enzymes

Once again, do not misunderstand this list. It does not assert that water is dominantly First Ray. We are thinking here of certain qualities it possesses : its necessity for life, its neutrality, its power of bringing all sorts of substances into intimate contact in solution, its incompressibility and great stability under different physical conditions, its erosive power and effect upon landscape, its transparency to light. So also with blood, which possibly belongs to another Ray, but has the red colour of the ruby and rushes freely where it can give itself in service, and therefore is here put as typical of the utter self-devotion, the fiery *tapas* of the Sixth Ray.

Suppose we turn now to sound, especially as produced in music, and follow the same method. This is a little more difficult. We have to concentrate on primary features of the instruments and of the sounds they produce : it will not do to think only of modern European instruments and the parts they play in an orchestra. Here is one classification :

1st Ray .... CYMBALS, gongs, explosions
2nd Ray .... FLUTES
3rd Ray .... REEDS, voice
4th Ray .... DRUMS, tympani
5th Ray .... HARPS, plucked strings
6th Ray .... BRASS
7th Ray .... VIOLINS, bowed strings

As a final illustration we may take a subtler series of subjects. Most of us have felt that the medium used in sculpture has some influence on the impression we receive. Marble, granite, bronze, wax, clay —each can express best certain aspects of the subject modelled in them because each has individual capacities in the way of hardness, uniformity of texture, weight, tensile strength, translucency, and so on.   A sculptor might model with infinite care an aeroplane in granite, or, as we have seen in industrial exhibitions, a statue of some celebrity in butter ; yet it is not mere association of ideas that makes the incongruity and unpleasing effect we feel in looking at such eccentricities.   Grace in execution, sureness of touch in modelling, must be wedded to fitness for use, and the latter is dependent upon what we may conveniently call the " life " of the material.   Let us try our Ray classification upon typical materials for plastic art :

1st Ray .... GRANITE, communicating strength, mass, reserve of power, nobility.

2nd Ray .... IVORY, communicating purity, impersonality, firmness, u n i t y, synthetic completeness.

3rd Ray .... MARBLE, communicating mobility, music, proportion, tenderness of bounding surfaces.

4th Ray .... ALABASTER, communicating inner life, sensitiveness, human feeling, responsiveness, ideality.

5th Ray .... BASALT, communicating precision, coldness, dignity, truth, purpose, symmetry.

6th Ray .... WOOD, communicating frankness, power, eagerness, humility, quiet stability.

7th Ray .... BRONZE, communicating rhythmic grace, time, measured force, elasticity.

Note that the last method involves the use of a prepared mould, and recollect that all ceremonial is the preparing of a mould for a psychic and psychological influx.

Having worked out several lists, the reader is advised to place them in tabular form side by side, and to try to find a connecting sympathy running across the horizontal columns.

It seems utterly crazy to wander from sapphire to milk, flutes and ivory, from topaz to honey, harps and basalt, but—try ! After all, there *is* honey in basalt if you look closely enough : honey-yellow crystals of olivine. We find the same recognition of the abstract unity behind the special senses in the application of painting terms to music and *vice versa*. In Emerson's words :

> Then we see that things wear different names and faces, but belong to one family ; that the secret cords, or laws, show their well-known virtue through every variety,— be it animal, or plant, or planet—and the interest is gradually transferred from the forms to the lurking method.

RAY	JEWELS	FLUIDS, etc.		SOUNDS	PLASTIC ART IN	COLUMNS
1.	Diamond	Water		Cymbals, gongs, explosions	Granite	Doric
2.	Sapphire	Milk		Flutes	Ivory	Ionic
3.	Emerald	Sea-water		Reeds, voice	Marble	Corinthian
4.	Jasper	Albumen	{ sperm and ovum	Drums, tympani	Alabaster	Egyptian
5.	Topaz	Honey	{ pancreatic juices	Harps, plucked strings	Basalt	Tuscan
6.	Ruby	Blood		Brass	Wood	Gothic
7.	Amethyst	Wine	{ hormones enzymes	Violins, bowed strings	Bronze	Caryatid

CHAPTER IV

STONES OF THE FIRST RAY

DIAMOND—ROCK CRYSTAL—TENTATIVE ADDITIONS :
WHITE QUARTZ, MAGNETITE, ZIRCON, OPAL

DIAMOND

Chemical composition : Carbon
Specific gravity : 3·4—3·6
Hardness : 10
Crystal system : Cubic (Isometric tetrahedral)

" A LITTLE diamond is worth more than a rocky mountain," observes old Burton, and no doubt the diamond has been prized from the earliest times, occurring as it does in natural octahedral forms which can be mounted without cutting. The art of cutting and polishing it, which greatly enhances its brilliance and sparkle, is said to have been discovered in 1496 by Louis de Berquem, although engraving on diamonds had been practised earlier.

4

The hardest of minerals, it has a name in Hebrew derived from the word for a hammer, because the diamond crushes and grinds all other stones. It has phosphorescent properties, being luminous in a dark room after exposure to sunlight, and also on friction. Subjected to electrical bombardment in a vacuum tube, it shines with a vivid green light.

There is a whole literature about diamonds, and many curious and fascinating histories attached to individual jewels, like the unlucky Hope diamond. Among the large number of old beliefs regarding the occult properties of this stone we need note only some which accord with the influence of the First Ray. Rueus ascribes to it the power of driving away troublesome dreams and unreasoning fears, of withstanding injury from enemies, and of maintaining unity and love :

> He who carries the diamond upon him, it gives him hardiness and manhood, and it keeps the limbs of his body whole. It gives him victory over his enemies in court and war, if his cause be just, and it keeps him that bears it in good wit . . . And if any cursed witch or enchanter would bewitch him . . . all that sorrow and mischance shall turn to the offender, through virtue of that stone.[1]

To the present writer the diamond seems to belong to an older evolution than that of this earth.[2] It has

---

[1] Maundeville.

[2] Note the occurrence of diamonds in meteorites.

a rich, exotic magnetism with the feeling of immense stability that arises from many ages of expression in this form. The colour-impression communicated by the life of the diamond is a deep indigo or indigo-violet.

There is an old tradition that diamonds could be made to grow, and the writer of *The Travels of Sir John Maundeville* unblushingly affirms that he has made the experiment. In the course of a lengthy account of the properties of the diamond, he says :

> And although men find good diamonds in India, yet nevertheless men find them more commonly upon the rocks in the sea, and upon hills where the mine of gold is. They grow many together, one little, another great, and there are some of the greatness of a bean, and some as great as a hazel nut. They are square and pointed of their own kind, both above and beneath, without work of man's hand ; and they grow together, male and female, and are nourished by the dew of heaven ; and they engender commonly and bring forth small children that multiply and grow all the year. I have oftentimes tried the experiment, that if a man keep them with a little of the rock, and wet them with May-dew often, they shall grow every year, and the small will grow great ; for right as the fine pearl congeals and grows great by the dew of heaven, right so doth the true diamond ; and right as the pearl of its own nature takes roundness, so the diamond by virtue of God, takes squareness.

The mysterious Comte de St. Germain evidently could at least improve diamonds by·removing flaws and impurities, if he did not actually make them grow.

Writing to Count Von Lamberg about his second visit to the East (1755-56), he remarks :

> I am indebted for my knowledge of melting jewels to my second journey to India. On my first expedition (1737-42) I had but a very faint idea of this wonderful secret, and all the experiments I made in Vienna, Paris, and London, were as such worthless.

In more recent times, Madame Blavatsky performed the feat of duplicating jewels. Here is Colonel Olcott's account of the production of a yellow diamond at Simla in 1880.

> We were dining at home that day and Mrs. Sinnett, H.P.B. and I were waiting for Mr. S. in the drawing-room. The ladies sat together on a sofa, Mrs. S. holding H.P.B.'s hand and admiring for the twentieth time a lovely yellow diamond ring that had been given the latter by Mrs. Wije-ratne of Galle on the occasion of our visit that same year. It was a rare and costly gem, full of sparkle and light. Mrs. Sinnett was very anxious that H.P.B. should double it for her some time, but she had not promised. Just now, however, she did it. Rubbing two fingers of the other hand to and fro across the stone, she after a moment paused and lifting her hand exposed the gem. Alongside it, lying between that finger and the next, was another yellow diamond, not so brilliant as hers, yet a very fine stone. It is, I believe, still in the possession of our kind and dear friend.[1]

Colonel Olcott explains this as an apport with the aid of the elementals of the mineral kingdom.

The artificial production of diamonds is a process of great scientific interest, although the result may be

[1] *Theosophist*, xvii, 196.

of no commercial value. The crystalline form of carbon which we call diamond can be got from charcoal if we can liquefy it and allow it to cool under very great pressure. The following diagram expresses

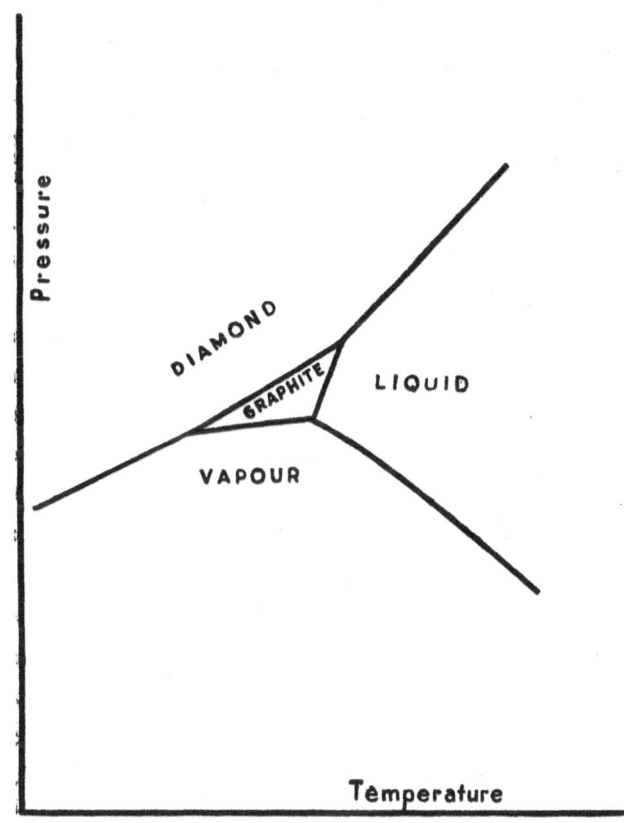

DIAMOND

GRAPHITE

LIQUID

VAPOUR

Pressure

Temperature

FIG. 2

in graphic form the relation of the various states of the element carbon to the temperature and pressure required to produce them.

The vertical direction represents increase of pressure and the horizontal increase of temperature. We see at a glance that carbon vapour can exist only below a certain pressure : above that pressure any increase of temperature will produce only hotter and hotter liquid at an enormous pressure. We see also that only under great pressure will liquid carbon solidify nto the diamond form instead of the commoner graphite.

Now several molten metals, notably silver and iron, dissolve carbon and deposit it in the crystalline form of graphite on cooling. The problem is, to add sufficient pressure to bring the condition of the cooling carbon into the area represented on the left of the diagram. It is solved as follows. Half a pound of very pure iron (free from sulphur, silicon, and phosphorus) is mixed with charcoal in a carbon crucible and put in an electric furnace. Two carbon poles make an electric arc over the crucible, transmitting 700 ampères at 40 volts pressure, and raising the temperature to over 4,000 degrees Centigrade. A few minutes at this very high temperature, and the iron is a glowing liquid saturated with dissolved carbon. The crucible is then held under cold water until it cools below red heat. The effect of this sudden chilling is to solidify the outer layer of the iron while the inner mass is still liquid. But since iron in passing from the liquid to the solid state expands considerably, the inner liquid, pent in by the crust around it, sets up a pressure of many tons to the square inch as it cools, and the carbon crystallises out under the pressure that was wanted.

Afterwards the metal has to be dissolved away by a mixture of hot nitric and hydrochloric acids, leaving the carbon behind. Most of it is in the form of graphite, but there are also translucent chestnut-coloured flakes, carbonado or black diamond, and a few crystalline fragments of colourless diamond. For the most part the true diamonds obtained by this process are mere tiny grains, suitable only for mounting on microscope slides.

ROCK CRYSTAL

Chemical composition : SiO_2
Specific gravity : 2·5—2·8
Hardness : 7
Crystal System : Hexagonal (trigonal)

Rock crystal is the pure, transparent and crystalline form of the mineral silica. Silica plays a large part in rock-building, and in various degrees of purity and tinted by different colouring matters forms the essential basis of dozens of types of stone, semi-precious, ornamental, or merely useful, like the flint.

Crystal is found chiefly in the older crystalline and granitic rocks. Its typical shapes are (1) six-sided prisms acutely terminated by six planes, (2) six-sided pyramids, (3) six-sided prisms with a six-faced pyramid at each end. Sometimes the crystals are quite large ; a two-foot specimen was found at Invercauld, near Braemar, Scotland. Rock crystal is widely distributed throughout the world, but the finest examples have been found in the Alps, Pyrenees, Siberia, Brazil, Ceylon and Madagascar.

Two pieces of rock crystal clashed together in the dark show faint flashes of phosphorescent light, or rubbed hard together give a pale yellow light. The electrical poles of the crystal are at the ends of the three lateral axes. Some of the ancients believed that crystal was a kind of petrified ice, and Sir Thomas Browne devotes a section of his book on *Vulgar Errors* to considering the old proposition " That Crystal is nothing else but Ice strongly congealed."

It is one of the seven precious substances of Buddhism, and in the Tibetan system the eastern region of heaven is built of white crystal. One of the attributes of certain of the Hindu gods is the *Akshamala*, or rosary of 24 crystals, representing the 24 Tattvas.

Owing to its hardness and beautiful transparency, and the circumstance of its being obtainable in considerable pieces, this material was worked into cups and vases from an early period, especially among the Greeks and Romans. Later, complete finger-rings were carved from it, or little caskets, and in the middle ages it was found useful for reliquaries. In the Waddesdon Bequest Collection in the British Museum there is a low vase and cover, with four diamonds set in the foot, which bears on its side in Arabic script the name of the Emperor-Adept of Hindustan, Akbar the Great (1542-1605).

In occult history rock crystal has always been a famous material for scrying or crystal-gazing ; not only does it provide the necessary " clear deep," but its elemental essence possesses qualities which are distinctly stimulating to clairvoyance (C. W. Leadbeater). A popular idea of this quality appears in Japanese folk-lore in the following recipe :

Take a block of crystal of the best quality. Hollow it out on the top and fill the cavity with quicksilver. Place this against your forehead and you will see wonderfully well in the dark.[1]

In the Scottish Highlands many crystal charm-stones were preserved for healing purposes. The usual practice was to apply to the patient—human or animal—water in which the stone had been dipped.

The psychic atmosphere of crystal has the characteristic stability note of the First Ray, but is very different from that of the diamond. One might describe it as unintelligent and sleepy, massive rather than focussed. There is also the quality of fire, but it is the homely glow of wood-embers in contrast to the electrical fire of the diamond. It is definitely part of our Mother Earth, and a rather undeveloped part.

TENTATIVE ADDITIONS

WHITE QUARTZ

Chemical composition : SiO_2
Specific gravity : 2·5
Hardness : 7
Crystal system : Hexagonal (trigonal)

---

[1] *Folk Lore,* xxxiii, 193.

This rock actually differs little from the more prized rock crystal.   Its opacity and white colour are due to the inclusion of innumerable minute bubbles or cavities containing either gas or fluid, and it is crystalline in its structure.   It is one of the typical constituents of true granites.

" Granite cannot burn, because its aura is Fire," says H. P. Blavatsky, and this rock has always impress- ed intuitive writers with a sense of power.   Victor Hugo[1] exclaims, " si le granit avait un coeur, quelle bonté il aurait ! Eh bien, le génie est du granit bon. L'extrême puissance a le grand amour."   And Emerson rhapsodizes :

Man, made of the dust of the world, does not forget his origin ; and all that is yet inanimate will one day speak and reason . . . Shall we say that quartz mountains will pulverize into innumerable Werners, Von Buchs, and Beau- monts ; and the laboratory of the atmosphere holds in solution I know not what Berzeliuses and Davys ?[2]

MAGNETITE

Chemical composition : $Fe_3 O_4$

Specific gravity : 4·9—5·2

Hardness : 5·5

Crystal system : Cubic

[1] *William Shakespeare.*
[2] *Uses of Great Men.*

This iron-black mineral occurs in grains and crystals in many rocks, and often forms beautiful octahedra reminding one of two Egyptian pyramids placed base to base. It is, of course, the Lodestone, or magnetic iron-ore, the mysterious Bone of Horus of the Egyptian mysteries, and it radiates the stability note of the First Ray.

ZIRCON

Chemical composition : $ZrSiO_4$
Specific gravity : 4·2—4·86
Hardness : 7·5
Crystal system : Tetragonal

The zircon or jargon usually forms square prisms, but sometimes pyramids, and varies from colourless through shades of yellow and orange to reddish-brown and smoky brown. The clear gem-variety is of a transparent orange or red or brown tinge, and is known as Hyacinth. The zircon has a brilliant lustre approaching that of the diamond, but is somewhat brittle and not so hard. It comes chiefly from the alluvial sands of Ceylon, from the gold regions of the Ural Mountains, and Laurvik in Norway. Its key-note might be described as independence or self-dependence.

OPAL

Chemical composition : SiO_2, perhaps H_2O
Specific gravity : 1·9.—2·3
Hardness : about 6
Crystal system : None—amorphous

This familiar and beautiful stone is a humble oc-
cupier of vacated tenements, forming in cavities in
certain types of lava, and sometimes replacing wood.
There is a clear glass-like variety called Hyalite, but it
is typically bluish with opalescent lights.   Held to the
light and looked through, it is brownish in colour.

The opal entices you away from everyday affairs to
an ideal world, a world of far horizons and high
purpose, and this impersonality of outlook is repellent
and " unlucky " to those of us who are not prepared
to sacrifice the personal for an ideal.

CHAPTER V

STONES OF THE SECOND RAY

SAPPHIRE—LAPIS LAZULI—TURQUOISE—SODALITE—TENTATIVE
ADDITIONS : BENITOITE, FLUORITE

SAPPHIRE

Chemical composition : Al_2O_3.
Specific gravity : 4
Hardness : 9
Crystal system : Hexagonal

CORUNDUM or aluminium oxide is the Chemical
composition of the sapphire, which is sometimes
reckoned to be the most beautiful in colour of all
precious stones. Strangely enough, however, the
blue colour is due to traces of foreign matter, so that
green, yellow and colourless sapphires occur, and the
same stone with a rich red hue we call the ruby.
It comes from the gravels of Burma, Siam, and
Ceylon.

The old lapidaries distinguished the rich, deep blue gems as male sapphires, and the pale blue as female. After subjection to intense heat the sapphire becomes snow-white. Exposed to the electric discharge in a Crookes tube it phosphoresces with an intense blue light.

It was believed to be a preservative against enchantment, " a great enemy to black choler, frees the mind, mends manners." The bed-frame of the mythi cal Prester John was of fine sapphires blended with gold to make him sleep well. It was also thought to be a powerful influence for purity and continence, and thus was, and is, regularly used in ecclesiastical rings by bishops and cardinals.

There is in the British Museum a figure of the Lord Buddha cut in sapphire, which recalls some remarks of Madame Blavatsky :

The marked respect [1] paid by the Buddhists to the sapphire-stone—which was also sacred to Luna in every other country—may be found based on something more scientifically exact than a mere groundless superstition. They ascribed to it a sacred magical power, which every student of psychological mesmerism will readily understand, for its polished and deep-blue surface produces extraordinary somnambulic phenomena . . . Thus Amoretti's investigations of the electric polarity of precious stones show that the diamond, the garnet, the amethyst, are — E while the sapphire is + E . . . An old Hindu legend says that Brahmâ-Prajâpati,

[1] *Isis Unveiled*, I, 264-5.

having fallen in love with his own daughter *Ushas* (Heaven, sometimes the Dawn also), assumed the form of a buck (ris'ya) and Ushas that of a female deer (rohit) and thus committed the first sin. Upon seeing such a desecration, the gods felt so terrified, that uniting their most fearful-looking bodies—each god possessing as many bodies as he desires—they produced Bhûtavân (the spirit of evil), who was created by them on purpose to destroy the *incarnation* of the first sin committed by Brahmâ himself. Upon seeing this, Brahmâ-Hiranyagarbha repented bitterly and began repeating the Mantras, or prayers of purification, and in his grief dropped on earth a tear, the *hottest* that ever fell from an eye; and from it was formed the first sapphire. . . . The Buddhists assert that the sapphire produces peace of mind, equanimity, and chases all evil thoughts by establishing a healthy circulation in man . . . " The sapphire," say the Buddhists, " will open barred doors and dwellings (for the spirit of man) ; it produces a desire for prayer, and brings more peace than any other gem ; but he who would wear it must lead a pure and holy life."

The hot tear of Brahmâ very curiously brings to mind modern experiments in the artificial production of sapphires, for it is precisely by heat that tear-drops or *boules* of sapphire have been made. The earliest attempts were made by allowing the vapour of aluminium fluoride to act upon boron anhydride at a high temperature, and it was claimed that very small blue crystals had been obtained. About 1908, however, M. L. Paris made other experiments, of which the following is a convenient summary.

When alumina is fused in the oxyhydrogen flame it becomes transparent, yielding a crystalline product to which a red colour is readily imparted by the addition of a little chromic oxide.   The mass is not coloured blue, however, by oxides of cobalt and iron, since these remain on the surface as a fused layer, while the interior remains colourless.   But if a trace of lime be present in the alumina, diffusion of the oxides occurs and the whole fused mass may be coloured blue by the addition of various metallic oxides, especially that of cobalt.   The artificial sapphires thus obtained consist of amorphous corundum, with a crystalline surface layer, and, as regards their physical characteristics, stand in the same relationship to the natural stones, as does fused silica to quartz.   They are exceedingly hard, and of a rich blue colour, and are not easily distinguishable, even by experts, from natural sapphires.

Later experiments achieved still better results by carefully dropping pinches of the appropriate mixed powder through an electric arc, the fused product collecting in an oval or pear-shaped drop below the flame.   This method gives a homogeneous mass throughout, but it still contains stress striations due to the piecemeal building-up of the drop, and these can be detected optically even when the synthetic material has been cut as a gem.

Mention may be made of the " Star sapphire." This is a stone with a peculiar internal structure due to repeated twinning of the crystal, so that actually what seems one crystal consists of a great number occupying the same space, like the medieval schoolmen's conception of a host of angels standing upon the point of one needle.   As a result of this phenomenon there are, parallel to the six sides, rows of infinitesimal

5

spaces or tubes which reflect light faintly. When a
stone of this type is cut *en cabochon*, that is, with a
plain, rounded surface like the end of an egg, the
star is seen to best advantage. If you bring a lighted
candle towards it, you see a glimmering star " as of a
white spider creeping round a world of its own, always
revolving and never coming to an end, resting sometimes, but, as soon as you with your moving light start
in pursuit hurrying on again." [1]

LAPIS LAZULI

Chemical composition : Silicates of Aluminium and
   Sodium, Sodium sulphide and sulphate, some
   Calcium.

Specific gravity : 2·3—2·45

Hardness : 5·5

Crystal system : None—amorphous, essential constituent, lazurite, is cubic.

Rich blue, azure, violet-blue and greenish blue are
the usual colours of this ornamental stone, known from
the most ancient times. Sometimes it seems speckled
with gold, although the yellow metallic particles are
not gold but the humbler mineral, iron pyrites. It is
found, chiefly in crystalline limestones, in various parts
of the East—Persia, Bokhara, Siberia, and China. It

[1] C. R. Ashbee.

appears from Pliny's description that this is the stone which the classical writers called *sapphirus*.

Lazuli is one of the seven precious substances of Buddhism ; some of the Babylonian cylinders are cut in it ; and in ancient Egypt, where it was called Khesdeb and Qesonkh, it was used a great deal in the manufacture of amulets and symbols. The Egyptians carved from lapis lazuli the cartouche, figures of goddesses, the Utchat or Eye of Horus, and the Sam and Shen symbols. It was a favourite material for statuettes of Isis.

The powdered lapis—the ultramarine of the older artists—figured in ancient medicine as an external dressing for boils and ulcerations, and internally as a purge and remedy for melancholy.

It is curious that lapis lazuli should be tied up with sex symbolism in different civilisations. In Assyrian texts there are references to the *salla* (pudendum) of Istar carved in lazuli, and to the " flute " of Tammuz in the same material. The Egyptian Sam symbol, already mentioned, represented the male organ. In Huysmans' extraordinary novel *Là-Bas*, the priest-occultist, Dr. Johannes,[1] diagnoses psychological cases by means of precious stones, and in the story lapis lazuli detects psychic disturbance due to incest.

[1] In real life the Abbé J.-A. Boullan of Lyons, who died in 1893.

TURQUOISE

Chemical composition : Hydrous phosphate of Aluminium coloured by a Copper compound.

Specific gravity : 2·6—3

Hardness : 6

Crystal system : None—amorphous

Though not a transparent stone, turquoise takes a fine polish which brings out its clear colour of sky-blue, bluish green or apple green. It comes from Naishapur, the Megara valley of Sinai, Turkestan and Tibet. A greenish variety is found in New Mexico, supposed to be the *chalchihuitl* of the ancient Mexican tribes, and this colour, which Pliny calls *callaina*, was most prized by the ancient Romans. In ancient Egypt the turquoise was called Mafkat of Amen, to distinguish it from Mafkat of Syria, which was malachite.

Its colour depends largely on the presence of water in the stone, for it dries to a dirty green colour, and can be restored by burying it for a time in moist earth.

The Tibetan turquoise or Bodhitse is one of the standard materials for rosaries and figures largely in folk-lore. There is the tale of a celebrated Tibetan physician who was presented by the gods and demons with an immense quantity of turquoises and other precious stones, which they heaped on the roof of his house.

SODALITE

Chemical composition :
A felspathoid, $Na_4 (AlCl) Al_2 (SiO_4)_3$
Specific gravity : 2·2—2·4
Hardness : 5·5—6
Crystal system : Cubic

This is not a traditional gem-stone, but rather an almost microscopic constituent of some trachytic lavas, appearing as colourless or blue cubes or rough grains scattered through the rock.   It occurs chiefly in south Portugal, Italy, Sicily, and Transylvania.   In recent years, however, it has been found in Maine, in Ontario, and on the Ice River in British Columbia, in large masses of sky-blue colour, and has come into use as an ornamental stone.

TENTATIVE ADDITIONS

BENITOITE

Chemical composition : $BaTiSi_3 O_4$
Specific gravity : 3·65
Hardness : 6.5
Crystal system : Hexagonal

Benitoite is a new gem-stone, chemically a titano-silicate of barium, and derives its name from the place of its discovery in 1907 near the headwaters of the San Benito River in California. It varies from colourless to deep sapphire blue, and having a high refractive power, makes a very brilliant cut stone.

The mineral life of benitoite is vivid but somewhat undeveloped. It seems to be a kind of terrene understudy to the older sapphire, which it may one day replace.

FLUORITE

Chemical composition : CaF_2
Specific gravity : 3—3·2
Hardness : 4
Crystal system : Cubic (isometric)

Fluor-spar occurs with various colourings from glassy transparence to blue, pink, and, rarely, red. Typically it is a handsome violet-blue, sometimes called " Blue John," and is found in beds and veins, often in association with metallic ores, especially lead ores. It is common in Saxony, and in the mining districts of England, especially Derbyshire and Cornwall.

Fluorite phosphoresces when heated, and has the remarkable property of transmitting exceedingly short waves of ultra-violet light.

Psychically it gives a dull atmosphere of peace, with little or no stimulative effect.

CHAPTER VI

STONES OF THE THIRD RAY

EMERALD—AQUAMARINE—JADE—MALACHITE—TENTATIVE
ADDITIONS : PRECIOUS OLIVINE, AMAZONSTONE, IRON PYRITES

EMERALD

Chemical composition : 3Be O. Al_2 O_3 $6SiO_2$
Specific gravity : 2·7
Hardness : 7·5—8
Crystal system : Hexagonal (rhombohedral)

THIS is the most precious form of the mineral beryl, that which is a deep, transparent green. Its six-sided prisms are usually marked lengthwise with fine grooves or striations, and it is found either in druses or cavities in granite gneiss, or embedded in mica-schists and chlorite-schists. In its most famous locality, however, Muzo in Colombia, it occurs in a black lime-stone. Peru, Brazil, Bavaria, India and Siberia are also notable sources of the emerald, and in ancient times it was mined in Egypt. Sir John Maundeville remarks that " in Egypt . . . abundance of fair emeralds are found, which are on that account cheaper than elsewhere."

The famous eye-glass of Nero is believed to have been an emerald :

> The deep-green emerald, in whose fresh regard
> Weak sights their sickly radiance do amend.[1]

Ancient authors describe columns and statues of emerald of immense size. Pliny cites Apion on the subject of a colossal emerald statue of Serapis in the Egyptian labyrinth thirteen and a half feet in height. It seems likely that these were really glass imitations. On the other hand it must be remembered that the common beryl—opaque or muddy green—has been found in truly gigantic crystals weighing up to two and a half tons, and possibly similar finds were the basis of the stories mentioned.

Burton remarks that " Mercurialis admires the Emerald for his virtue in pacifying all affection of the mind." In Egypt the papyrus-sceptre amulet, symbol of vigour and renewal of youth, was usually fashioned in mother-of-emerald, or light green porcelain.

[1] Shakespeare, *A Lover's Complaint.*

AQUAMARINE

Aquamarine differs from the emerald only in colour : it is a bluish-green transparent beryl. Good stones are found in Brazil, Siberia and India.

It has been mounted and engraved from early times, and according to Buxtorf, is the " beryl " mentioned in Exodus, xxviii, 20. Pope Julius II wore an aquamarine, over two inches long, in his tiara. This stone was taken away by the French, but later restored to the Papal See by Napoleon.

JADE

Chemical composition : Silicate of Aluminium and Calcium.

Specific gravity : 3—3·2

Hardness : 6

Crystal system : Monoclinic

True jade, or nephrite, must be distinguished from another mineral loosely called by the same name, the silicate of aluminium and sodium, or jadeite.

Jade is a tough material which takes a good polish, and is typically of a dark leek-green colour, and somewhat soapy to the touch.

We associate jade particularly with China, where it has always been put in the first rank of precious stones, and where so many masterpieces of patient carving in it have been made ; but in other localities where the Atlantean stock survived we find jade playing a prominent part. The Aztecs, who assigned green to loyalty, worked jade ; the lake-dwellers of Switzerland (Tlavatlis) had jade axe-heads; in the Amazon valley, in Brazil, where no jade occurs naturally, great numbers of amulets and axes of this material have been found ; and in New Zealand, " poenamu " is carved into figures, hatchets and axes. It was the Nemehen of ancient Egypt.

In 1905 Mrs. Conger, wife of the American Minister, was presented by the Empress Dowager of China with a blood-jade as an amulet for her safe return to America. " The stone had been worn by some one of China's rulers for two thousand years, and the present Empress Dowager had worn it during her reign, during the siege of 1900, in her flight, during her stay hundreds of miles from her palace home, and during her return to her own Peking and Forbidden City, and it had protected her through all dangers. This protecting power she wished to go with me in my journey homeward. My gratitude was great, and my reply sincere." [1]

[1] S. P. Conger, Letters from China, 353.

MALACHITE

Chemical composition : $CuCo_3 . Cu(OH)_2$
Specific gravity : 3·7—4
Hardness : 3·5
Crystal system : Monoclinic

Green carbonate of copper, which is supposed to be named from the Greek *malache*, " marsh-mallow," is a fairly widely distributed mineral, rarely found in translucent crystals, but more usually in pearly or silky-looking emerald green masses, often fibrous in structure.

Since it can be obtained in slabs it has been much used as an ornamental stone and inlay for tables. Its most ancient use, however, seems to have been as a cosmetic. In the prehistoric period of Egypt it was ground along with galena (lead sulphide) on slate palettes, and this powder, mixed with water, was painted on the eyelids. In later Egyptian times it was the amulet material called Mafkat of Syria.

Malachite is a mineral of relatively quick formation. Recent sea-shore sands exist which have the particles coated and bound by this mineral (Wheal Leisure), and bronze objects have been found at ancient Assyrian sites partly or wholly converted into malachite.

PRECIOUS OLIVINE

Chemical composition : $(MgFe)_2 SiO_4$.
Specific gravity : 3·3—3·4
Hardness : 7
Crystal system : Rhombic

Olivine is a common constituent of certain types of rock, but is most frequently altered and decomposed until it appears almost grey-black. Occasionally occurring in clear, glassy, yellow-green crystals which can be cut and polished as gems, it shows well in artifical light, and has been called the "Evening Emerald," also the Peridot or Chrysolite.

AMAZONSTONE

Chemical composition : $K_2O. Al_2O_3.6SiO_2$
Specific gravity : 2·57
Hardness : 6
Crystal system : Triclinic

This is a bright green variety of the felspar Microcline, sometimes used as an ornamental stone.

IRON PYRITES

Chemical composition : FeS_2
Specific gravity : 4·9—5·1
Hardness : 6—6·5
Crystal system : Cubic

Pyrites is a common constituent of rock-masses, and, although an ore of iron, is more frequently used as a source of the sulphur with which it is combined. Its glittering greenish-yellow cubes are familiar to us in roofing slates, and it also gleams in household coal— "brasses" as they are called by the coal miners. The name is derived from the Greek *pur*, "fire." The Cornish copper miners call it *mundic*.

In the island of Elba iron pyrites has been found in large pentagonal dodecahedrons, *i.e.*, twelve-faced crystals, each face having five sides.

CHAPTER VII

STONES OF THE FOURTH RAY

JASPER—CHALCEDONY—AGATE—SERPENTINE—TENTATIVE
ADDITIONS : PEARL, MOONSTONE, SELENITE, ALABASTER

JASPER

Chemical composition : SiO_2, with various colouring
    matters.
Specific gravity : about 2·6
Hardness : 7
Crystal system : Cryptocrystalline

JASPER, the chief stone of the Fourth Ray, has
many . varieties and colours, although a bright red
might be said to be typical. Green, yellow, pink,
black, and bluish colours have been used as gem-
stones, and from Siberia we have the striped riband
jasper ; from Egypt another sort with concentric
zones of different brown hues. It occurs widely
throughout the world, but in addition to its most

famous source, Egypt, the ancient specimens were derived mostly from India, Persia and Cappadocia.

Red was associated with Isis as the Mother of magnetic life, and the amulet formed of the buckle of her girdle was frequently carved in red jasper, which the Egyptians called Khenem. The amulets of the serpent's head and of the sacrificial cow were also fashioned in it. There is in the British Museum a square signet of yellow jasper with the name and titles of Amenophis II.

Many of the Assyrian and Babylonian cylinder seals were engraved in this stone ; green jasper scarabs of Phoenician origin have been found in Sardinia ; and Maundeville refers to a box of green jasper which was in the Ark of the Jews.

Dioscorides mentions jasper as particularly suitable for the making of amulets. A great number of the so-called Gnostic gems—the *abraxas*—are engraved on this stone ; but it should be noted that Abraxas or '' Abrasax, the Great God of the ignorant, was placed among the lower hierarchies of the Gnosis, and the popular idea of him was assigned to the lowest building powers of the physical body.'' [1]

Geometrical patterning is characteristic of the Fourth Ray, as in Egyptian art, and it is interesting to

[1] Mead, *Fragment of a Faith Forgotten*, 283.

see this quality objectively manifested in the rhythmical banding and lining of many jaspers. In imitation of the mineral, we have in architecture diaper-work (Italian, *diaspro* ; Latin, *diasprus*, " jasper-like ") where a conventional pattern of flowers, leaves or scrolls, is enclosed in repeated small frames fitted regularly together ; and the same idea has been carried into textiles, where diapers have a pattern of geometrical regularity.

One doubts whether jasper is really the highest mineral development of the life of this Ray, since it is not a pure crystal type ; on the other hand, the Fourth Ray, as a bridge or balance Ray between the three abstract and the three practical Rays, may require just such a structure, crystalline only in its minute parts.

CHALCEDONY

Chemical composition : SiO_2
Specific gravity : about 2·6
Hardness : 7
Crystal system : Cryptocrystalline
This again is one of the forms of the Protean mineral silica. A waxy-looking bluish white stone which takes a brilliant polish, it really consists of

6

intermingled layers or fibres of crystalline quartz and amorphous silica or opal. It varies through shades of blue-grey to brownish, and in its basest form becomes flint and chert, and is found in the hollows of lavas and limestones as a secondary formation.

It has been polished and engraved from early times for seals and reliefs. With the Egyptians the amulet of the heart was frequently carved in it ; while from classical times we have the engraved chalcedonies of the Dionysiac Bull by Hyllus, and the Medusa of Solon—both typical of the downard-tending life of the lower worlds. Burton says of it :

> There is a kind of Onyx, called a Chalcedony, which . . . avails much against phantastick illusions which proceed from melancholy, preserves the vigour and estate of the whole body.

AGATE

Chemical composition : SiO_2 with colouring matter

Specific gravity : about 2·6

Hardness : 7

Crystal system : Partly cryptocrystalline

The river in Sicily anciently called Achates is said to have given its name to this stone, since fine varieties were found on its banks. The agate is a variegated stone resulting from the deposition of silica from solution in zones and bands in the hollows of igneous rocks.   In one pebble or nodule there may be a large number of concentric layers of different states of quartz, chalcedonic, jaspery, and crystalline, coloured principally in shades of red and brown by iron oxides. When the pebble is cut through and polished, the beautifully regular system of lines and bands is shown up, and when these have a zig-zag outline like the plan of a military fort, the stone is called a " fortification agate."   Moss-agates are so called because they show vegetable-like branching structures running through the pebble.   Localities are, Egypt, Greece, Arabia, Uruguay, and the trap-rocks of Scotland.

The agate was considered a charm against scorpions and spiders, and a talisman for athletes.   Sir Thomas Browne mentions the belief that " the fume of an agate will avert a tempest," which would be indeed characteristic of the Harmony Ray, though how agate could be made to yield a " fume " is not explained. The great Teacher of the Fourth Ray, Orpheus, " did commend the stone called an Agate."

Apart from the geometric patterns, to which we have referred under Jasper, the agate also shows the remarkable imitative faculty of this Ray, for in many instances it replaces wood fibres cell by cell and part by part, so that we have an imperishable reproduction in agate of prehistoric plant forms.   This replacement extends to the microscopic structure of the vegetable matter ; and although wood-opal is commoner, wood-agate is a finer reproduction of the original.   There is a story that about the year 1760 the Emperor of Germany, being desirous to know the length of time necessary to complete a petrifaction, obtained leave from the Sultan to take up and examine one of the timbers that supported Trajan's bridge over the Danube, some miles below Belgrade.   The outer part of this timber to the depth of half an inch was found to be converted to an agate ; the inner parts were slightly petrified ; and the central were still wood.

SERPENTINE

Chemical composition : $2H_2O. 3MgO. 2SiO_2$
Specific gravity : 2·5—2·65
Hardness : 3—4
Crystal system : Monoclinic

The mineral serpentine is a rather soft, slightly translucent, yellowish or greenish granular substance found chiefly in limestones ; but the name is more commonly applied to the rock-masses of altered minerals with serpentine as their main component.

Massive serpentine is spotted and veined in a manner resembling the markings of a snake's skin, and usually contains in addition to serpentine, lime carbonate, steatite or soapstone, or diallage, or dolomite. In colour it is generally a rich green or red, permeated by veins of whitish steatite. Some varieties have a base of olive green with bands or blotches of brownish red, or bright red, mixed with lighter tints ; or olive green with steatite veins of greenish blue ; some are red studded with veins of green diallage ; some clouded, and some striped (Spon). An exceptionally hard type of green serpentine is carved in Afghanistan where it is regarded as jade. Serpentine is found at Portsoy in Banffshire, Lizard Point in Cornwall, Canada, Siberia, Galway in Ireland, Egypt, and Italy.

The Ophites or Serpent-stone of the ancients came from the neighbourhood of Memphis. In the Cairo museum there are two fine statues about three feet high carved in serpentine and representing Osiris and Isis enthroned. They were found in the necropolis of Memphis, and are attributed to the XXXth dynasty. The oldest gems from Assyria are cylinders of serpentine one or two inches long and half an inch thick, pierced though their long axis for a cord to attach to the wrist.

CHAPTER VIII

STONES OF THE FIFTH RAY

TOPAZ—CITRINE—STEATITE—TENTATIVE ADDITIONS : CAIRN-
GORM, AMBER, CHRYSOTILE, OBSIDIAN, JET

TOPAZ

Chemical composition : $Al_2 SiO_4 (F,OH)_2$
Specific gravity : 3·5
Hardness : 8
Crystal system : Orthorhombic

THIS brilliant and beautiful stone occurs in quartzose
rocks ; also in association with tin ores, and in some
gravels as rolled pebbles. In colour it is usually
either limpidly transparent or tinged with various
shades of yellow. Some of the tinted varieties are
made pink by heating, and rose topaz, natural or
artificially induced, goes very well with gold, especially grey gold. A noteworthy variety is the sky-blue
topaz found in the Scottish Highlands, suggesting the

hard-headed type of religion characteristic of the Scot ; that is, the Fifth Ray of science (topaz) with the Second Ray of religious intuition (blue colour). The chief localities for the gem topaz are Brazil and Siberia, and also Saxony ; though good specimens are obtained in the Mourne Mountains and in Colorado.

Topaz was supposed to assist the virtue of fidelity in friendship. Other properties are summarized by Burton in his *Anatomy of Melancholy* thus : " The same properties I find ascribed to Jacinth and Topaz, they allay anger, grief, diminish madness, much delight and exhilarate the mind. If it be either carried about, or taken in a potion, it will increase wisdom, saith Cardan, expel fear ; he brags that he hath cured many mad men with it, which, when they laid by the stone, were as mad again as ever they were at first."

CITRINE

Citrine or " false topaz " is merely rock crystal of a bright yellow colour. It is, of course, not quite as hard as topaz, and not so brilliant in its refractive power.

There is in the famous Townshend collection a remarkable piece of quartz carved as a monkey's face, one half of the stone being citrine and the other pink quartz. Maundeville has a curious statement that "yellow crystal draws colour like oil."

STEATITE

Chemical composition : $3MgO. H_2O. 4SiO_2$.
Specific gravity : 2·8
. *Hardness* : 1—3.
Crystal system : Probably monoclinic

Steatite, soap-rock, or soapstone, is a massive form of the mineral talc—familiar in its cut or powdered form as "French chalk." It is exceedingly soft and easily carved or turned, and distinguished by its soapy feeling to the touch. It is found in localities where serpentine occurs, of which rock it often forms a considerable constituent.

The Egyptians used it extensively as a material for seals and intagli, and in India and China it is still used as a material for carving. In modern times it has been used for many more or less prosaic purposes associated with *fire*, for it has fire-resisting qualities. In the early years of the nineteenth century twelve tons of steatite were raised annually in Cornwall for porcelain manufacture. In the United States a steatite paint is made and applied to ships' bottoms, to walls for preventing dampness, and to roofs for making them fireproof.

CAIRNGORM

This typically Scottish stone, deriving its name from the Highland mountain *massif*, is a tinted variety of rock crystal, differing from citrine only in its paler yellow colouring, or in possessing a brownish tinge in the deeper yellow specimens.

It is still a favourite ornamental stone for the brooches and dirk-handles worn with Scottish Highland dress.

AMBER

Chemical composition : Carbon, hydrogen and oxygen ; allied to succinic acid.

Specific gravity : 2—2·5

Hardness : about 5

Crystal system : Amorphous

The conifers of the Tertiary period exuded the resins which, fossilised in lumps and fragments, we call amber. Usually pale yellow in colour, it varies through orange and red shades to an opaque brown ; more rarely it is found white, greenish, bluish, or violet. Its chief locality is the Baltic coast between Konigsberg and Memel, but it also occurs in Sicily (a fluorescent variety called Simetite), the Adriatic, Siberia, Greenland, the United States, Burma, and Australia. The New Zealand " gumcopal " is a softer, less fossilised type.

Amber has been prized from prehistoric times, as is proved by the ornaments found in the early burials and lake-dwellings of Europe. It has long been regarded as a charm against disease and infection, and this was the idea behind its introduction as a material for mouthpieces. A volatile oil can be distilled from it, which was believed to be of value in infantile convulsions.

In Mohammedan countries it is esteemed as an incense as well as for talismanic properties. The Shah possesses " a cube of amber, which, we are told, fell from heaven in Mohammed's time. It is supposed to render the Shah invulnerable, and he wears it about his neck." [1]

The use of amber in the varnish is said to have been one of the master secrets of the makers of the famous Cremona violins.

[1] Grant, *Mysteries of All Nations*, p. 636.

CHRYSOTILE

Chrysotile, which must be distinguished from chrysolite (see under " Precious Olivine "), is a pale-yellow fibrous variety of serpentine, similar to asbestos. The stone, however, which we have particularly in mind here, is a hard type coming from South Africa, which also contains some quartz and takes a good polish. It shows a series of lustrous lines and bands of golden-yellow and brown strongly reminiscent of spectrum photographs.   This stone is known as Crocidolite and is somewhat different in chemical composition from its ally, Chrysotile, and is a favourite material for " cat's eye " ornaments.

OBSIDIAN

Volcanic Glass is another name for this ancient cutting-tool material. It is a dark brown or black glassy rock formed by the rapid cooling of acid igneous masses.

Knives, spear-heads and axes were chipped out and polished in this stone by many savage races. The ancient Mexicans used it for sacrificial knives, and the Egyptians fashioned in obsidian the amulets of the Two Fingers, the Double Feather, and the Sma

sign of Union.   Classical literature records the dedi-
cation by Augustus to the temple of Concordia of
four obsidian elephants, and also mentions an obsidian
statue of Menelaus belonging to Heliopolis.

Like thought, at first fiery and fluid, this rock sets
hard, then gradually crystallizes : masses occur where
the stages of the passage from the vitreous to the
crystalline state can be studied under the microscope.

JET

Synonym for blackness, jet might be called the
precious variety of coal, for it is a hard resinous
variety of lignite, or carbonised wood.

The Greeks, who got it from Syria, believed that
powdered jet was a remedy for toothache.   Many
early European burials have been found to contain
ornaments of jet.

Whitby in Yorkshire, where the jet occurs in Upper
Lias shale beds, was once an important centre for
jet-working, but most of the material is now collected
in France and Spain.

CHAPTER IX

STONES OF THE SIXTH RAY

RUBY—TOURMALINE—GARNET—CARNELIAN—CARBUNCLE
—THULITE—RHODONITE—TENTATIVE ADDITION :
RED CORAL

RUBY

Chemical composition : $Al_2 O_3$
Specific gravity : 4
Hardness : 9

EXCEPT in colour, the ruby is physically identical with sapphire, being a crystalline corundum or aluminium oxide. It is, however, usually a little softer than the sapphire, and is a scarcer and more valuable stone. The chief source is the gem-sand of Burma (Mogok), Siam and Ceylon, but crystals are also found *in situ* in some altered limestones.

After exposure to sunlight the ruby phosphoresces in the dark for a few moments, and in the electric discharge in a vacuum tube glows red.

It is one of the seven precious substances of Buddhism, and the western region of the Tibetan heaven is composed of Pemaraga, or ruby. That delightful romancer who wrote *The Travels of Sir John Maundeville* did not forget the ruby among the other wonderful stones he describes. Writing about Nacumera, the isle of the dog-headed people, he says that their king " beareth also about his neck an orient ruby, noble and fine, which is a foot in length and five fingers large. And when they choose their king, they give him that ruby to carry in his hand, and so they lead him riding all about the city. And that ruby he shall bear always about his neck ; for if he had not that ruby upon him they would not hold him for king. The Cham of Cathay has greatly coveted that ruby, but he might never have it, neither for war, nor for any manner of goods." Elsewhere he tells us that the great Khan has a ruby half a foot long.

Mediæval writers ascribed to the ruby the power of curing or bringing forgetfulness of evils springing from friendship or love.

The English Rosicrucian philosopher, Fludd, has some interesting references to this stone. " The red earth," he says, " of which Adam was formed, had in it the virtue of the Sephiroth ; it was, therefore, matter pure and good—a ruby or carbuncle gem."

In his *Tractatus Theologo-Philosophicus* (1617) he apostrophises the Lord Christ : " O Ruby ! whose blood is the salvation of the faithful ; O Carbuncle ! who by Thy splendour and clearness illuminates mankind."

TOURMALINE

Chemical composition : $H_9 Al_3 (B. OH)_2 Si_4 O_{19}$; H being replaced by Al, Na, Mg, Fe.

Specific gravity : 3—3·3

Hardness : 7—7·5

Crystal system : Hexagonal (trigonal)

Precious tourmaline occurs in light and dark blue, green, red and yellow colours, but here we are concerned with the red and pink varieties, distinguished as Rubellite or Siberite (from Siberia).

Tourmalines are obtained from Elba, Maine, Siberia, Ceylon and Brazil, and are found in elongated crystals in number of rocks both igneous and metamorphic. This mineral is as nearly opaque to heat as alum, and becomes electrified under its influence, one end of the crystal becoming positive, the other negative.

There is something reminiscent of the one-pointed *tapas* or devotion of the Sixth Ray in the tourmaline's property of absorbing light and conducting electricity best in one direction only, that is, at right angles to the optic axis of the crystal.

GARNET

Chemical composition $\begin{cases} 3 \text{ FeO. Al}_2\text{ O}_3. \text{ 3 SiO}_2 \\ \text{(Almandine).} \\ 3 \text{ MgO. Al}_2\text{ O}_3. \text{ 3 SiO}_2 \\ \text{(Pyrope).} \end{cases}$

Specific gravity : 3.7—4·3

Hardness : 6·5—7·5

Crystal system : Cubic

The garnets are a fairly large family of stones varying from white through yellow, red, apple green and brown, to black.   Under this Ray we are dealing with the transparent red and purple-red types, known as pyrope and almandine.   They are found in round grains or dodecahedral crystals.

The blood-red pyrope occurs in serpentine rocks or alluvial deposits in Bohemia, Saxony, South Africa, Santa Fé and Ceylon.   The purplish red almandine is found in various schists and altered rocks, or in gravels from these, as in Ceylon.

Garnets were favourite ornamental stones in the later days of the Roman Empire, and among the

Celtic and Anglo-Saxon tribes. Burton includes it in his catalogue of antidotes to melancholy : " Granatus : a precious stone so-called because it is like the kernels of a Pomegranate, an unperfect kind of Ruby, it comes from Calicut; if hung about the neck, or taken in drink, it much resisteth sorrow, and recreates the heart."

CARNELIAN

Carnelian is a red-tinted chalcedony, or more or less transparent silica with colouring due to iron oxide. Lapidaries, however, extend the name to cover all the semi-transparent varieties of chalcedony ranging from yellowish white through yellow, red and brown to grey-black. The transparent red type is called Sard, carnelian being somewhat clouded. The best specimens come from Arabia, India, Mesopotamia, Surinam and Siberia.

Early Etruscan and Egyptian scarabaei are found in this stone, and it was also used by the Egyptians (who called it Hersed) for a number of amulets : the Heart, the Buckle of Isis, the Eye of Horus, the Nefer, the Serpent's Head, and the Sun's Orbit. In classical times it was frequently employed for engraved gems with martial subjects. In Buddhism it is one of the seven precious substances.

7

Madame Blavatsky gives an interesting account of the carnelian which she wore.[1] '' The talisman,'' she says, '' is a simple agate or carnelian known among the Thibetans and others as *A-yu*, and naturally possessed, or had been endowed with very mysterious properties. It has a triangle engraved upon it within which are contained a few mystical words.''   And she adds in a footnote : '' These stones are highly venerated among Lamaists and Buddhists ; the throne and sceptre of Buddha are ornamented with them, and the Taley Lama wears one on the fourth finger of the right hand. They are found in the Altai Mountains, and near the river Yarkuh. Our talisman was a gift from the venerable high-priest, a *Heiloung* of a Kalmuck tribe.''

CARBUNCLE

Carbuncle is a name given to almandine garnet when it is cut and polished *en cabochon*, that is, like a rounded button without facets. A piece of foil is set at the back to throw out the light, producing a rich fiery red effect.

There was a curious belief that the carbuncle emitted light of its own. No doubt this was in Fludd's

[1] *Isis Unveiled*, II, p. 599.

mind when he addressed Christ as the " Carbuncle, who by Thy splendour and clearness illuminates mankind." Maundeville in his description of Prester John's bedchamber introduces carbuncles as a suitably exotic illuminant : " All the pillars in his chamber are of fine gold with precious stones, and with many carbuncles which give great light by night to all people. And although the carbuncle gives light enough, nevertheless at all times a vessel of crystal, full of balm, is burning, to give good smell and odour to the emperor, and to expel all wicked airs and corruptions."

Not unnaturally the *carbunculus*, literally " a little coal," was used sometimes for the eyes of images or carvings intended to be awe-inspiring, as in the case of the Baphomet of the Templars, or the shield of Sir Thopas in the *Canterbury Tales* :

> His shield was all of gold so red,
> And therein was a boare's head,
> A carbuncle beside ;
>
> And there he swore on ale and bread,
> How that ' the giant shall be dead,
> Betyde what betyde ! '

The carbuncle looks well set in ivory, but in modern times has fallen out of favour : " the fairy carbuncle which nobody will wear because it is so cheap—the dear good parsons, kind, innocent men, preferring the imitation glass carbuncle at four times the cost." [1]

THULITE

Chemical composition : a basic orthosilicate of the epidote group, Ca_2 (Al. OH) Al_2 $(SiO^4)_3$
Specific gravity : 3·25—3·37
Hardness : 6—6·5
Crystal system : Orthorhombic
Thulite occurs in granular masses at Piedmont, Italy, and in the granites of Svuland in Norway. It is a rare and fragile variety of the mineral epidote, in colour ranging from peach-blossom to rose red.

RHODONITE

Chemical composition : MnO. SiO_2
Specific gravity : 3·4—3·6
Hardness : 5·5—6·5
Crystal system : Triclinic
This mineral—a red triclinic pyroxene—derives its name from the Greek *rhodon,* " a rose," but it is also known as Manganese Spar and Paisbergite. Its shades are light brownish red, flesh red, rose pink, and dark

[1] C. R. Ashbee, *Art Journal,* 1894.

rose red.   It is found in the iron ore beds of Sweden, in the Ural Mountains, in Piedmont, Hungary and Mexico ; also along with lead and silver ore at Broken Hill, New South Wales.

It is sometimes cut and polished for ornamental inlaid work, and has also been used to give a violet colour to glass.

TENTATIVE ADDITION

RED CORAL

Although, like the pearl, coral is a product of the animal kingdom, it undoubtedly calls for some notice as a stone.

The Romans and the Greeks alike used it for decorating their weapons, partly because of its talismanic properties, and in the East it has always been a favoured material for necklaces.   In Renaissance times in Europe red coral was used for ornamenting church vessels, and down to modern days the peasantry in many parts of Europe have believed in a sprig of coral as a protection against the evil eye.

Paracelsus, after describing Phantasmata or " Shells," says " they are afraid of red corals, as dogs are afraid of a whip," and he " recommends the wearing of red corals as a remedy against melancholy. They are said to be ruled by the influence of the sun, while those of brown colour are under the influence of the moon. The red ones are disagreeable not only to Phantasmata, but also to Monsters, Incubi, Succubi and other evil spirits." [1]

[1] Hartmann, *Paracelsus*, p. 108.

CHAPTER X

STONES OF THE SEVENTH RAY

AMETHYST—PORPHYRY—VIOLANE—TENTATIVE
ADDITION : HAEMATITE

AMETHYST

Chemical composition : SiO_2
Specific gravity : 2·5—2·8
Hardness : 7
Crystal system : Hexagonal

AMETHYST is identical with Rock Crystal except for
its colouring, which ranges from pale purple to deep
violet-blue. The violet colour is supposed to be due
to a trace of manganese or of ferric acid. When the
stone is cut with a great number of facets, the depth
of the colour of an amethyst is intensified, and is
beautiful in a setting of silver or pale gold : with yellow

gold it looks vulgar.   Finely coloured amethysts are found in India, and dark specimens in Brazil ; other localities are Ceylon, Persia, United States, Spain, Siberia, Arabia Petraea, and Armenia.

It was known as Sef Tahen in ancient Egypt, and in classical times was much used for intagli, especially of Bacchanalian subjects.   There is a fine intaglio head of Pan in an Italian collection.   Its Hebrew name, according to Aben Esra, is derived from its power of bringing dreams and visions to the wearer.   James III of Scotland, depressed at the spectacle of his sons in arms against him, donned an amethyst signet ring on which was carved a fading vine surrounded by waves which were supposed to be wine, not water, with the engraved motto : *Mea sic mihi prosunt* (Thus are mine to me).

The name is usually interpreted as from the Greek, *a*, " *not*," and *methystes*, " drunkard, " and is held to refer to the belief that this stone had the power of preserving its wearer from excess in drinking.   It may be suggested, however, that this was a popular interpretation of teaching given in the Mystery schools.   The name " unintoxicated " referred to the quality which the Seventh Ray man possesses of evoking and transmitting powerful invisible forces without losing his self-control and equilibrium.

PORPHYRY.

This deep-red rock came into favour in classical times because in colour it was near the imperial "purple," which of course was not our purple, but a deep crimson colour with only a touch of purple in it. Busts of emperors were made of porphyry, with the head added in marble.

The typical porphyry is of a beautiful red colour with thickly scattered oblong crystals of white felspar. It is very hard and takes a fine polish. The original porphyry came from Jebel Duchan in Upper Egypt, and is the rock called hornblende-porphyrite. Porphyry is found in Britain in Aberdeenshire and Cornwall, and in many other parts of the world.

Talismans were cut in this stone by the later Romans, and it was also used as an art material by the Italian Renaissance engravers. In modern times it was used for the sarcophagi of Wellington and Napoleon. The block which was used for Wellington's tomb was taken from a moor in Cornwall, and took two years to hollow out and prepare. Napoleon's porphyry resting-place is cut from still greater blocks of this enduring stone ; it is said the lid alone weighs thirty-two tons.

VIOLANE

Chemical composition ; CaMg $(SiO_3)_2$, with Manga-
nese.
Specific gravity : 3·2—3·3
Hardness : 6
Crystal system : Monoclinic

Violane is named from its violet colour, and is a
form of the pyroxene Diopside.   It is a mineral with a
waxy lustre, usually occurring in layered masses, sometimes fibrous, and occasionally in prismatic crystals
of a dark violet-blue which are only translucent, although transparent in thin sections.   Its chief locality is St. Marcel in the valley of Aosta in Italy, where it
occurs in small seams along with quartz and silicates in
the rock called braunite.

TENTATIVE ADDITION

HAEMATITE

Chemical composition : Fe_2O_3
Specific gravity : 4·5—5·5
Hardness : 5·5 —6·5
Crystal system : Hexagonal (trigonal)

One of the common ores of iron, haematite has
many forms, fibrous, massive, earthy, and crystalline,

and its colour varies slightly according to the type of structure, from steel-grey to shining iron-black, and in the earthy form deep red.

Some of the Babylonian engraved seal-cylinders are of haematite. The Egyptians, who called it Qo or Qada, used it for a number of important amulets : the Utchat, the pillow or head-rest, the square, the level, and the " two fingers "—index and medius— which Horus used in assisting his father Osiris up the ladder into heaven.

NOTES

First Round and Archetypes, page 24 :

It is interesting to copy for comparison a passage from Fludd's *Mosaicall Philosophy*, which was first published at Gouda in 1638, then in English translation in London, 1659. " For whatsoever was originally decreed in the secret counsell of the Archetype is affected from a generality into many specialities, and from each speciality unto an infinite number of individuall particularities ; so that the Æviall or Angelicall effect is the image of the externall Idea, and the temporall world is the similitude of the Æviall ; and again, in the temporall or typeical world, every stellar shape is the likeness or paterne of the Angelicall Idea ; and again, the Elementary things are the shadows of the Spiritual Shapes or Images in heaven."

Permanent Atom, page 28 :

Victor Hugo in his *William Shakespeare* has a curious passage where he associates the soul with an atom. Roughly translated, it runs thus : " Why not great souls amongst humanity like great trees in the forest, great peaks upon the horizon ? We see great souls as we see great mountains. Well then, they exist. But here questioning persists—anxious questioning. Whence come they ? What are they ? Who are they ? Are there some atoms more divine than others ? That atom, for instance, which will be dowered with the power of irradiation here below—this one which will be Thales, this which will be Æschylus, this which will be Plato, this which will be Ezekiel, this Maccabaeus, this Apollonius of Tyana, this Tertullian, this Epictetus, this Marcus Aurelius, this Nestorius, this Pelagius, this Gama, this Copernicus, John Huss, Descartes, Vincent de Paul, Piranesi, Washington, Beethoven, Garibaldi, John Brown,—

all these atoms, souls holding sublime office among men, is it that they have seen other worlds and bring thence the essence to earth ? Who sends the master minds, the guiding intelligences ? Who determines their appearance ? Who is the judge of the real need of mankind ? Who chooses the souls ? Who sounds the call to the atoms ? Who decrees the departures, who premeditates the arrivals ? "

The Seven Sacraments, the Planets, Jewels and
Rays, page 42 :

It is instructive to compare the assignation of the planets, jewels and sacraments as given by Eliphas Levi in his *Rituel de la Haute Magie* (p. 115) with C. W. Leadbeater's list of jewels. Arranging Levi's data so that the planetary rulers corresponded to the Rays in so far as their influences are appropriate in this case, we have :

1. Sun	Holy Orders	Chrysolite, ruby.
2. Moon	Baptism	Pearl, crystal, selenite.
3. Jupiter	Holy Eucharist	Emerald, sapphire.
4. Venus	Holy Matrimony	Turquoise, lapis lazuli, beryl.
5. Mercury	Confirmation	Agate.
6 Mars	Penitence	Amethyst.
7. Saturn	Extreme Unction	Onyx.

Materials of Sculpture, page 46 :

After these pages were written, the writer came across Stanley Casson's *Some Modern Sculptors* (Oxford and London, 1928) which contains in the first chapter a very notable discussion of the various materials of sculpture. " Basalt," he says, " can give a particularly lovely surface, as can be seen in a portrait-head by Mestrovic, but it is a thankless medium."

The Soul of the Diamond, page 50 :

Victor Emile Michelet, in his witty little book *L'Amour et la Magie* (Paris, 1909), has a poetical and intuitive passage on the nature of the diamond : " The soul of the diamond is a more impenetrable thing than the darkest recesses of the soul of woman.   How can we know its psychology when its anatomy is a mystery? Newton and Lavoisier gave up its analysis.   It seems a sublime substance, invisibly pure, impassively lofty. Petrified light, solidified phosphorescence, spiritualised ice ; for it is all coldness as it is all splendour. No substance can scratch it, no emotion seems to have the power to penetrate it.   It lives in pure intellectuality, dead to all feeling, to all passion, like a heart which, plunged in the Absolute, has become divested of both tenderness and hatred.   Indomitable, the ancients called it,—Adamas.   It is also called the Solitary One.   Isolated in the consciousness of its strength and pride, no magnetic currents are able to penetrate it ; it intercepts them.   The alchemists were of the opinion that it, among all the stones, had reached the summit of nobility and beauty, as gold had among the metals, and the sun among the planets.   And so they included among their symbols the Schamir, the mysterious and unique diamond whose possession opened for Solomon, Prince of the Magi, the golden gates of the totality of knowledge."

Jade in Ancient Mexico, page 75 :

This was really jadeite, usually showing rather regular dark mottling or flecking on a lighter ground of dull blue-green. Prescott, in *The Conquest of Mexico*, says : " After the lapse of ten days the Mexican envoys returned,   They entered the Spanish quarters with the same formality as on the former visit, bearing with them an additional present of rich stuffs and metallic ornaments, which, though inferior in value to those before brought, were estimated at three thousand ounces of gold.   Besides these, there were four precious stones, of a considerable size, resembling emeralds, called by the natives chalchuites, each of which, as they assured the Spaniards, was worth more than a load of gold, and was designed as a mark of particular respect for the Spanish monarch.   Unfortunately they were not worth as many loads of earth in Europe."   A footnote adds that the use of this stone was permitted only to persons of rank, who wore it attached to the wrist by a thread as a token of their nobility.

INDEX

Printed by C. Subbarayudu at the Vasanta Press, Adyar, Madras.